Return Journey

RETURN JOURNEY

Fred Noonan

The Book Guild Ltd.
Sussex, England

The Book Guild Ltd
25 High Street,
Lewes, Sussex

First published 1994
© Fred Noonan 1994
Set in Baskerville
Typesetting by Ashford Setting and Design Services
Ashford, Middlesex
Printed in Great Britain by
Antony Rowe Ltd
Chippenham, Wiltshire.

914·2

A catalogue record for this book is available
from the British Library

0863 329 098 1107

ISBN 0 86332 909 8

CONTENTS

In Memory.

To John Ruddy, father-in-law, confidant, much loved friend. Deceased 27th February 1991. Always the first to express joy at our successes, comfort at our failures. Someone whose love and humility was always a source of motivation. We felt you with us John.

Faltering Steps

It was 21 May 1990.

'I feel as if we have only come half way,' said Joan. After months of planning, weeks of effort and 1027 miles of walking we had arrived at John o'Groats. Joan was feeling the emptiness of anti-climax, the ending of a dream. I was struggling with a different sort of emptiness. After a thousand mile walk to the pub we had arrived just in time to hear last orders being called. I arrived at the bar with eleven seconds left and ordered drinks all round. As Joan and I were the only customers and the barman couldn't understand English this was a cheap round. However, even after the necessary refreshment and sustenance the emptiness wouldn't go away. Joan was right. It did seem only half way. As we left John o'Groats the following day the thought of a return journey gradually took hold.

Joan does not like walking. The walk to John o'Groats was partly due to a promise made many years ago through the bottom of an empty beer glass. I was with my wife Joan in the saloon bar of the King's Head, near Lancaster. I had just started a new job in Weston-Super-Mare 250 miles away and was commuting weekly, just coming home at weekends. This meant that each seven days of living were having to be compressed into one precious weekend. It was whilst preparing for yet another house move during one of those precious weekends that I found my old school atlas and, nostalgically looking through it, I came across a map of Great Britain with some lines drawn on it, relics of an earlier route planning attempt twenty-five years ago.

In the early sixties an eccentric peace campaigner and CND activist, Dr Barbara Moore, had captured the nation's imagination with some of the feats she got up to to bring

attention to her cause. One of her regular 'habits' was to walk
from Land's End to John o'Groats!

I had become particularly attracted to this novel way of seeing
Britain and for nine months I planned my attempt to emulate
the feats of Dr Barbara Moore. However, rock climbing was
my first love and two weeks before zero hour I aborted
everything in favour of accepting a place on a rock climbing
team setting off to attempt the ascent of one of Europe's last
great unclimbed rock faces. This in turn was aborted when, with
a week to go, one of the team members, a bright light of British
mountaineering, became a dim glow by falling off a bit of Welsh
rock, breaking a pelvis. With two great ambitions lying dead
in the street I then opted for a six week rock climbing holiday
in the Lake District.

The discovery of the atlas had reawakened my marathon walk
ambitions. As Joan and I enjoyed another precious weekend,
sitting in the saloon bar of the King's Head and sampling Clive's
excellent beer, I started to reminisce.

'I will be a happy man when I walk from Land's End to John
o'Groats,' I said. Joan rattled her empty glass impatiently as
I prattled on. 'Always wanted to do it,' I said as Joan went to
the bar, 'ever since I was sixteen....' I muttered to the empty
chair. 'Must do it before I'm too old...' as Joan came back from
the bar.

The night went on. Many refills later we had decided I would
do it as soon as I retired.

'You wait until then and I'll walk it with you,' Joan slurred.
'I don't really like walking, but if you do it, I'll do it!' she said
bravely, contemplating the bottom of her glass.

I could only marvel at the strength of Clive's beer. Both of
us, safe in the knowledge that my retirement was at least twenty
years away, began to plan the route.

The months rolled by. My new venture in Weston-Super-
Mare was doing well. My sons reached school leaving age and
left school as soon as they could! With school problems out of
the way, we made plans to move house and be a re-united family
again.

It was at this time I started to be bothered with a pain in my
left eye. At first I thought it was due to a blocked tear duct but
fifteen gallons of eye wash later and I was doubting my self-
diagnosis. As the frequency and severity of the pain increased,

I realised that really it was a sinus problem. I became a well-known customer at a popular chain store chemist. I almost became addicted to nasal sprays. I was eating tablets for sinus problems at a faster rate than they could be made. The atmosphere both at home and in the office began to resemble a tropical rainforest as I resorted to humidifiers and inhilations.

None of these self-cures worked. The attacks of pain increased to as many as six a day. With very little warning, ten minutes at most, I would find myself on the floor, screaming in agony as nerves behind my eye and down my face felt as though they were on fire. Often accompanied by vertigo and muscle weakness, for anything up to two hours at a time I was totally disabled by the most unimaginable pain penetrating every single nerve ending on one side of my face. At this point I was leading some very delicate complex negotiations to buy out our biggest competitor and my colleagues were becoming increasingly disturbed at the sight of me rolling on the floor at the most inconvenient moments. A difficult interview with the company chairman, a kindly man distantly related to Attilla the Hun, resulted in him telling me in the kindest possible way that when the negotiations finished I should get the problem sorted 'before the problem sorts me'.

I have always been reluctant to visit doctors but enough was enough. Two years after those first discussions with Joan in the King's Head I was with the consultant neurologist at my local hospital. I was invited to stay for a few days for 'tests'. Tests meant putting my head in a huge magnet (brain scan), having my nose squashed flat against X-ray machines (sinus X-rays), having my eyes poked out (pressure tests for glaucoma), being strapped to a board and swung around in a room (inner ear tests), having bright lights shone in my eyes (test for other brain diseases), taking pills that made me sick, pills that stopped me being sick but caused constipation, pills to make me go, pills to make me come back. I was eventually discharged long enough to be given a chance to recover my health before round two, the conclusive interview with the consultant.

'We don't fully understand it,' he said. 'Relatively benign IF we get it under control,' he said later.

I didn't think much of that word 'IF'.

'Pain is one of the most severe produced by the human body,' he continued.

I waited for the punch line. It was not long in coming.

'Of course, we have no cure and these attacks of disabling severe pain may well continue for the rest of your life.'

A few days later I was with the company chairman. 'What guarantee do I have,' he said gently at 120 decibels, 'that my group finance director, when asked by a shareholder to explain the company's profits, will not suddenly leap out of his seat, scream, and bang his head on the walls?'

I muttered something lamely.

'What guarantee do I have,' he thundered on, 'that my finance director, when asked by the bank manager for a cash flow forecast, will not suddenly fall to his knees, sobbing?'

I muttered something even more lamely whilst holding my head. There was no other course of action left to either of us. A vibrant, developing company cannot be driven along by someone likely to be disabled with pain at any time without warning.

I went home with a heavy heart. Joan, who was helping out at the local farm, had just come in after an arduous journey home from work, a 500 yard drive. As she waited I gave her the bad news. 'I've retired due to ill health,' I said.

Our world came to an end. For the next few weeks we were shattered. How does a workaholic come to terms with no work? How are dreams and plans, the basis of a happy partnership, restored against such a calamity?

It was Joan who broke the spell. Casting her eyes over the rows of gleaming, unused Ordnance Survey maps, she said, 'At least we can do the walk now.'

Even though we had planned a route, or to be more exact, lots of routes, there was still some extra planning to do. Our early thoughts did not include Sherry, our ten-year-old sheep dog. However, as we were starting roughly twenty years earlier than planned, she had to be part of the team. We had also originally planned to walk from one bed and breakfast establishment to another, essential items for comfortable living packed into a rucksack and a cast of thousands back home receiving parcels of dirty clothing, washing and repacking them and then despatching them to the next pick up point. My health problems now made carrying a heavy rucksack unattractive and the thought of taking our irascible, geriatric sheep dog walkies from one dog loving establishment to another made the whole idea impossible. The problem seemed insurmountable until Joan suggested the idea of a motor caravan. Being a self-contained home we could not only carry all our worldly goods with us, we could also carry Sherry as well.

This seemed a good idea at the time. All we needed was someone to drive it for us. Another month went by before a further flash of inspiration hit us. The idea took the material form of a pile of wet concrete dust on our new living room carpet. It had been deposited there by an eighteen-year-old youth called Iain, our son. He was working as a labourer on a building site and liked to take his work home with him, or at least parts of it, in the form of cement dust, dirty boots and overalls with bits stuck on them, guaranteed to cause multiple injuries to any washing machine with the bad luck to be given the hopeless task of getting them clean. Iain was waiting to join the army the following June. We really wanted him to join the army immediately but NATO was trying to give peace a chance for just a little bit longer.

'If Iain finished work in March, we could start the walk in April and still finish in time for June,' suggested Joan. We put the proposal to Iain who seemed to warm to the idea of driving a large, expensive vehicle. I was also pleased until I heard him drawing comparisons between a motor home and another large vehicle, an armoured one.

After six months of planning we set off on 23 March with Iain acting as a support team and the three of us plus Sherry packed into our newly acquired motor caravan which we termed our lorry. We had intended setting off on April Fool's day but impatience, bad weather and an unplanned-for level of unfitness persuaded us to bring our plans forward and give ourselves an extra week. Sixty days and many adventures later we had arrived at John o'Groats with our feet a little worse for wear, the lorry a little worse for wear and Iain very much the worse for wear, having been blamed for everything, including the weather.

As we returned home, heavy hearted at the end of a great adventure, we made an overnight stop at Aviemore. On average, there had been an incident involving the lorry every hundred miles. Now, over one hundred miles from John o'Groats and so far with a clear round we stopped, partly to break the journey home, and partly to celebrate Iain having driven the lorry for over one hundred miles without pranging it, breaking keys or losing whole sets of keys. That evening, sitting in a friendly pizza house in Aviemore, I could not help but notice the strange behaviour of a group of young people in the restaurant. As the evening wore on it became obvious that they were severely physically and mentally handicapped. If our hearts were heavy before that meal they were heavier afterwards as we came to realise what a privilege we had enjoyed. The ability to walk, to comprehend new vistas around us, to have ambition and the ability to achieve it, all the things that those young men and women would never have.

Back home, summer came and went and the possibility of a return journey depended on the lasting effects of the anti-climax we experienced in those first few moments of our arrival at John o'Groats. It takes a lot of time, a lot of planning and a lot of effort to do the walk. If you are a person who does not like walking it also takes a lot of courage. As 1990 closed we were no nearer to a final decision other than agreeing if we were to do the walk then it would be for charity.

We were introduced to the National Star Centre for Disabled Youth when we reached John o'Groats. In the 1970's a Bristol dentist, Bob Thornton, founded a club called the 'Jogle' Club, (from the initials John o'Groats Land's End). Membership is open to all who complete the journey either way by any means and the £5 membership fee goes as a charitable donation to the Star Centre. Bob founded the club after a series of walks took him from one end to the other and to date that remarkable man has raised over £100,000 for this worthy cause.

The aims of the Star Centre are to provide full time further education for severely physically disabled young people. Based near Cheltenham, the centre offers residential places for up to 120 students at any one time. It was originally set up in the 1960s following the Thalidomide tragedy but very soon, under the guidance of the Department of Education, a wider need was realised. Students come from all over the United Kingdom to benefit from the specialist facilities at the centre and increasingly students attending are the most severely disabled. For those young people the Star Centre is not just home. It is not just a college. It is a place where they can be equal amongst equals and fulfil a potential that in normal circumstances would never be achieved.

For two people realising the privilege of walking a thousand miles, the thought of helping those who will never have the opportunity was irresistible.

January 1991. We were at the Derwent Hotel, Torquay for the Land's End — John o'Groats Association annual dinner. Alcohol does not agree with the disease in my brain and I have to ensure that the right pills have been taken before I can drink. Consequently my opportunities for indulging are severely limited. This day was one opportunity. We had a few drinks before dinner. Over dinner the wine was found to be reasonable in both quality and price and a second bottle was ordered.

As the presentations started to take place I felt mellow and warm. Then I heard our names being called. Joan and I stepped forward. A certificate was put in my hand. I mumbled something and a microphone was put in the other hand. Joan groaned and looked skywards. The prayed-for divine intervention did not take place and I started to speak into the microphone. 'Fantastic walk, fantastic experience,' I started to bumble.

'Fantastic big mouth,' Joan thought as her eyes bored into the back of my head, trying to paralyze the speech centres. They failed. 'Immense feeling of anti-climax....' I bumbled on. Joan's eyes tried to paralyze everything. In Churchillian tones I started to talk about the Return Journey.

Joan, in desperation, looked for a table knife, hammer, thermic lance, anything that would silence the yakking menace by her side. 'Sponsored walk...National Star Centre...21 May on the anniversary...' I cried, reaching a Mussolini type climatic ending. Rapturous applause from a slumbering audience. Joan with her hands around my neck. We were committed.

From now on things went steadily downhill. Joan's father, seriously ill at the time of the dinner, steadily declined in health. Joan spent more and more time in Rochdale to be with him. Sadly, at the end of February he died.

In the meantime my disease got worse. I had been referred to a world famous specialist in London who had immediately instigated a massive increase in the dose of a wonder drug. I got worse. Seeing an international reputation slipping down the pan the world famous specialist further increased the dose. I found myself unable to keep awake, nauseous, too weak to even hold a pint glass. I was privileged to be a pall bearer at my father-in-law's funeral but struggled to hold the coffin. When we returned from Rochdale I went for blood tests and was told that I had sufficient wonder drug in my blood to kill one and a half people! It was many weeks before I was fully recovered from the effects of the inadvertent overdose.

It was now March. Little planning had been done and neither Joan nor I had any great enthusiasm. We still had our motor caravan but as Iain was no longer available, due to work responsibilities, we had to find others to act as a back up team.

Living in the close confines of a motor caravan is one thing when it is all family, with strangers it is entirely different. We decided right from the outset that additional accommodation would be necessary. We had been promised a caravan by a leading manufacturer but now they decided they couldn't let one go for so long. This bad news at the time seemed rather academic as the two friends who had agreed to act as a back up team had since decided they couldn't spare so much time.

We plodded on and slowly the enthusiasm returned. We were introduced to Andy, brother-in-law of a friend and an out of work chef. Andy offered to be one half of our back up team. Culinary expertise is not something Iain possesses in great measure and both Joan and I suffered from his attempts at home cooking. Andy's credentials as a chef endeared him to us straight away, even if he was a vegetarian.

To find a partner for Andy we placed an advert in a magazine for itinerant overseas travellers, people on working holidays. We had a huge response and with a large shortlist we arranged to meet prospective candidates somewhere in Earl's Court, that location being chosen due to the overwhelming contingent of Australasians on the shortlist.

Arriving at Earl's Court tube station shortly before the planned arrival of the first candidate, we looked for somewhere discreet to interview. Stomping from one café, pub and wine bar after another, most of them being full of stuffed koalas and lifesize kangaroo replicas, we eventually settled on an upstairs table in a burger bar that was only full of lifesize replicas of Australians.

Ordering a vast quantity of chips from one lifesize replica, we settled down to a day's interviewing. Twelve hours, fourteen cups of coffee and an indescribable quantity of burgers later we had found Zoe, a twenty-one-year-old Australian from North Queensland. Zoe's self-proclaimed abilities to do everything from driving fifty ton articulated lorries to performing open heart surgery with only a bush knife and mulberry leaves was taken with a pinch of salt but her ability to laugh, joke and take everything with a smile warmed her to us immediately. All we needed now was accommodation for the dynamic duo.

We started to hunt around for a second-hand caravan, good enough to last 2000 miles, comfortable enough to accommodate two people and a dog for six weeks and cheap enough to be able to afford it! A startled salesman at a nearby caravan dealers offered to do a good deal in exchange for publicity and nearly died when I insited on paying by Access. I reasoned that if we walked quickly enough we could get to Land's End and back again in time to sell the caravan before Access clobbered my bank account!

The previous year we had averaged twenty-one miles a day on the days that we walked, plus taking a further ten days for lorry repairs (pranged), keys cut (lost), foot repairs (blisters) and rest days. This year I decreed that our average including days off would be twenty-one miles, which in practice meant that we had to walk twenty-five miles each day to 'earn' the spare time for rest days, etc. This gave us a target arrival day at Land's End of 8 July. I also varied the route plan, in places making cosmetic improvements and in others making radical changes. In particular the stretch from Manchester to Okehampton would be all new ground.

We were all ready to go. The line up: Joan and me walking. Zoe and Andy backing up. A motor caravan (lorry) and a caravan towed by Joan's Land Rover Discovery. Ben (Andy's dog), Sherry (our dog), and Rocky (my son's dog).

Northernmost Britain

21 May 1991. We assembled at John o'Groats. Whilst the points Land's End — John o'Groats are the accepted points for anyone wishing to travel the length of mainland Britain, neither are at the geographical extremity. In the north, the bleak and uninhabited headland of Dunnet Head is a few miles further north than John o'Groats whilst to the south the southernmost point is the collection of cafés, souvenir shops and car parks known as Lizard Point. She who does not like walking had decided if we were going to be daft we might as well throw in Dunnet Head and the Lizard.

At Dounreay, near Dunnet Head, is the experimental fast breeder reactor. The nature of its work and the eerie appearance of its golfball shaped reactor buildings earn it the popular title of Doomsday. The previous day, as we stood at Dunnet Head, I thought Doomsday had already arrived. Dunnet Head might be the end of Britain but on bad weather days like this it can look like the end of the world. A cold wind tugged at our anoraks as I looked at the surroundings. The cold waters of the Pentland Firth surround a headland of crumbling cliffs topped by brown, bleak, waterlogged peat.

The first few miles from Dunnet Head are a study in desolation. Nothing lives on this windswept peninsular. There are no trees, just brown peat interspersed with cold-looking pools and lochens. After three miles the village of Brough is reached and for the first time green replaces brown as the principal colour. We also saw our first sign of life. The most northerly horse in Britain. I groaned inwardly, knowing what would happen next. Sure enough, Joan wandered over and after a five minute chat gave the most northerly horse the most northerly lunch, my apple.

Shortly after Brough the road joins the main A836 Thurso to John o'Groats road. We now tramped along that road as it skirts the most northerly coastline in Britain. The cold and blustery weather stayed with us as we walked the remaining twelve miles to John o'Groats, the wind reaching gale force at times. As we tramped the main road the castle of May, belonging to the Queen Mother, drifted in and out of the mist. John o'Groats, never the most welcoming place, looked more cold and uninviting than usual. We took the dogs with us for this short walk as we had plenty of time. Rocky, barely a year old and with boundless energy loved it. Ben enjoyed the company of the other two dogs. Sherry, the veteran of last year's great trek, plodded along with a resigned expression.

I was glad to reach the Land Rover and leave the coast. The weather was most uninviting and I hoped for better tomorrow. Back at the site in Wick, we had been assured by the site warden that this weather was unusual for the time of year. Looking forward to fish and chips that night we had been disappointed when told that the boats couldn't get out of Wick Harbour because of the high winds and there was no fish. We opted instead for a Chinese take-away. 'Hope the sampans made it!' commented Andy as we waited for a 35 and 47 with three lots of 24.

Now, as we stood having our photographs taken, the wind was rattling the souvenir signpost. It was a nostalgic moment. My mind drifted back to last year when we had stood under the same signpost. Then our thoughts were on the achievement of getting there, of ambitions realised and of great anti-climax. Now our thoughts were on the struggle ahead and would it all work with people that a few days ago were strangers to each other? At last the photocall was over. Zoe, Andy and the three dogs set off in the Land Rover to John o'Groats village three quarters of a mile away.

It was a moment not without trepidation. Would my health stand up to the stress? I was in a no win situation. The pills I took to keep the pain away had side effects, cramp in the legs, painfully numb feet and weak muscles being the most obstructive. Take too much medication and every step would be a struggle to overcome pain and weakness. Try to do without and it was to risk attacks of agonising pain. It was a fine balance. I had been cheered by the absence of symptoms the day before and reduced my intake of pills and potions to give my leg muscles a flying start.

For a few moments Joan and I stood there, alone with each other, alone with our thoughts, remembering the bad times and the good times last year and the complete confidence we had earned with each other. It was no reflection on our back up team but at that moment we both missed Iain.

Then we set off. At the top of the hill by John o'Groats village we were met by strong gusts blowing in our faces. We marched on. The most northerly part of Britain is a flat and featureless place composed largely of peat and heather. Few trees grow in this cold, windy climate. Whether the wind blows off the Atlantic or the North Sea there is nothing to break it blowing from one side to the other.

The wind got stronger. We reached the highest point for miles around, the 300 foot hill called Warth Hill, and the viewpoint known as Black Loch. Black Loch was white as we passed it, the wind whipping up a fine spray. We reached the Hill of Harley, another towering giant at just over 200 feet high. A couple of hundred yards after this windy height the road goes round a sharp right hand bend and we found ourselves being blown sideways.

Reaching the small village of Nybster we met Zoe in the Land Rover armed with sandwiches and tea. Grateful for shelter from the wind, we scrambled in and ate in silence, exchanging anxious glances each time a severe gust rocked the vehicle.

Refreshed, we left the Land Rover and waving a not too cheerful farewell to Zoe, set off for the remaining ten miles to Wick. The wind got stronger. Gusts were blowing us backwards and into the road. Had it not been the 21st, and all the nostalgia associated with that date, we would have given up. As the winds continued to increase we found ourselves having to sit down as traffic approached to avoid being blown into its path.

Two miles from Wick, my body informed me that my gamble with my health was about to backfire. The first signal was a sharp pain down the left side of my face. A few steps more and a searing pain over my left eyebrow informed me of the outbreak of World War Three in my head. A few more stumbling steps and my left eye felt as though it was on fire; pain was now engulfing my head. The shriek of the wind assumed deafening proportions as the pain rose to a crescendo. I sat down by the roadside; no good, had to keep going. I crossed to the shady side of the road. I held my hands to my ears to keep out the roar of wind and traffic. I closed my eyes to try and keep out the searing pain. I staggered a few more steps. Screams choked in my throat, a bench fortuitously came near. I sagged down onto it and held my head in agony, praying for quick relief, praying that the drug I always carried with me, that I had now breathed into my lungs via a medihaler, would soon relieve the searing agony that was engulfing my left eye and face. An hour passed, an hour that seemed like a lifetime, an hour of strength-sapping, agonising pain. Slowly the drugs began to work and the pain receded sufficiently to allow progress to be made. Gingerly, on legs shaking with exhaustion, I walked the final miles into Wick.

Our schedule demanded twenty one miles per day. So far we had done seventeen. We desperately wanted to start to walk on schedule but outside the wind seemed to be getting even stronger. Even Rocky had lost all interest in going walkies. Two hours went by. Two hours in which the wind rocked the lorry and caravan with such ferocity that Zoe, whose tropical home suffers normally with mere cyclones, was getting concerned and frightened. Two hours whilst the last vestiges of pain disappeared from my head and strength returned to my legs. At six o'clock Joan and I faced the inevitable. We were either going to start the walk behind schedule or get out there and walk four more miles.

We set off again into the teeth of the wind. If it had moderated slightly no one was letting on. Struggling to put one foot in front of the other we continued towards the village of Thrumster and its dreaded television mast. Coming the other way last year, we first caught sight of this tall obelisk from about ten miles away. Travelling over such flat terrain it was a question of once seen, never out of view. No matter which way the road went that dreaded mast, never seeming to get closer, was in our line of vision. It took about three hours to pass, by which time my sanity level, never particularly great, had sunk to jabbering idiot level.

Near to Thrumster and we reached Loch Hempriggs. Hardly of great scenic interest at the best of times, its black and forbidding appearance seemed almost evil as the wind blew a drenching spray into our faces. Struggling past the Loch we reached the dreaded mast. Not daring to look up and resume eyeball contact with that source of many nightmares, I kept my eyes firmly focussed on my feet. Passing motorists must have gazed with sympathy at the shuffling, hunchbacked gnome that struggled south that day.

We eventually reached Thrumster, where we were met by Andy in the Land Rover. Returning exhausted to the camp site we popped in to see the warden and collect a weather forecast.

'Not usually like this,' said the warden, trying desperately to keep his hut on the floor. 'Normally get sunny weather in May,' he grunted as his hut threatened to become airborne. That night we listened to the weatherman talk about gusty conditions in Scotland. The following morning we listened to the coastguard telling us that the winds averaged storm force 7, gusting to storm force 10 — 70mph straight into our faces! No wonder we were exhausted.

The following day our route was to take us to the small village of Berriedale, twenty-three miles away. Five miles from Thrumster and we were at a place called Bruan on the edge of a cliff falling steeply into the wind-whipped North Sea. Desolate except for a ruined chapel, this was nearly a scene of disaster the previous year. Joan had needed to obey the call of nature and stumbling amongst some ruins for a decent spot she was seized with a sense of foreboding so strong she stopped in her tracks, literally, with one foot still poised in the air. Looking down to where her foot would have gone she saw a large beam of wood with rusty six inch nails protruding, points upwards. One more step and those tetanus and other disease ridden spikes would have easily perforated the soft soles of her training shoes and embedded themselves deep into her foot.

The wind had moderated only slightly, blowing off the land in a westerly direction. We were glad to reach Bruan for a ridge of gently elevated land broke the wind, giving us a much needed respite. Six miles from Bruan and at the fishing village of Lybster we again emerged into the teeth of the wind. Needing a rest after the exhausting struggle, we made our way to the Portland Arms Hotel. With the wind to our backs, I pushed open the door just as an extra special gust blew. Coats flew off the hatstand, clouds of ash blew out of the ashtray and the barman disappeared in a snowstorm of lemon slices and stuffed olives. Having made a grand entrance we ordered fruit juice and sandwiches while customers helped the barman clear up the wreckage.

Refreshed we left the Portland Arms Hotel and set off once more for Berriedale. The last words we heard on leaving was the barman saying to another customer, 'I don't know what's wrong with the weather, it's not usually like this.'

'Personally I've never known it any different,' I said to Joan who was again disappearing into the snug confines of a blue anorak.

That morning I had swallowed enough pills to keep World War Three at bay and was now paying the price. Despite the rest my calf muscles had now settled into knots of cramp and it was a hobbling wreck that continued to make progress that afternoon.

Three miles from Lybster, near Latheron, is a farm gate with an ornamental arch made out of whalebones, the remains of a whale beached up on the coast a few years ago. As the wind almost blew me to a standstill I could only sympathise with the whale. I was beginning to think we wouldn't escape either and in a few years time our bones would be used to tart up another farm entrance.

We eventually reached Berriedale by the middle of the afternoon. It is an important place for the foot traveller. Berriedale Brae is a steep plunge into a wooded valley, followed by a steep climb out, and whichever way it is approached it is a strenuous, arduous place. From Berriedale onwards the terrain changed dramatically, from the flat and featureless to the hilly and mountainous. In Berriedale there is also Kingsparke Guest House where the weary traveller can get a bed or, if he wants to press on, a cup of tea or coffee. Whatever the requirement the traveller will always get the warmest welcome.

We dropped in to see Brian and Mary Gough at Kingsparke. 'Not usually like this,' said Brian, referring to the sullen skies and gusting winds. I was getting used to people trying to persuade me that Caithness is usually a worthy rival to the Costa Brava. 'Not good at all,' said Brian, holding on to a sturdy piece of fencing to keep upright.

'Certainly not good for whales,' I said, imagining a whole flotilla about to be blown into his car park. Even Mary Gough's llamas looked as though they were pining for the less harsh conditions of the high Andean ice cap.

We met Brian and Mary the previous year when travelling in the opposite direction. We had walked from Brora, twenty-five miles away. The next camp site was at Wick, twenty-six miles away. Either way, to camp meant a twenty-five mile drive. With the end so close I was desperate that nothing should go wrong on these last few miles of twisting road to either our lorry or the walking disaster area called Iain. In the absence of camp sites nearby I had decided that we stay in bed and breakfast for the night. We had already located a place with large enough grounds to park the lorry and we made our way there, looking forward to staying with a Highland couple. As they introduced themselves I blinked in astonishment.

'Where be you from then?' I said in my best Somerset dialect.

'I be from near Bristle, in Zummerzet,' said the man.

'Where in Zummerzet be that to then?' I asked.

'It be to Yatton, near the Mendips,' said the man.

Brian and Mary Gough had moved to Caithness the previous year. They bred llamas which apparently grow better in the colder, drier climate. I would have thought polar bears and timber wolves would grow well there as well but I think Mary preferred the more placid temperament of the South American beast of burden.

Refreshed by the warm hospitality offered to any traveller who takes the time to visit Kingsparke, we continued on our way. We wanted to get the dreaded Brae behind us before we finished for the day. Puffing and wheezing, we were met at the top of the steep hill by Zoe who took us to the camp site at Brora. I was grateful to see Zoe. The cramp in my legs was now reaching a crescendo and I doubt if I could have walked another mile. The wind had moderated slightly, from force 7 to a mere force 5. It was still cold and grey but the sun was promising to pay a visit. As the day drew to a close and we warmed ourselves in the snug confines of our lorry, I watched the weatherman on television pin sunny emblems all over the map and point arrows with numbers five to fifteen on them in every conceivable direction. 'Apart from the far north,' I heard him say as I gently started to doze. I opened one eye just in time to see him pin a big black blob roughly in the position of our motor caravan. 'Winds could be severe,' he said, as I opened the other eye in time to see an arrow with thirty-five on it get stuck into our black blob.

The black blob was duly in place as we set off from Berriedale back towards the camp site. Zoe had taken us along the windswept shore and in dismal silence returned us to our finishing point from the day before. We even tried to negotiate with Zoe on the precise location but she wouldn't listen. 'Rules are rules,' she said in the sort of voice that would strike terror into the heart of any aboriginal bushman. 'You start from the exact point where you finished the day before. NO CHEATING,' she emphasised. Reaching the top of the Brae she kicked us out of the Land Rover and, in a cloud of black diesel smoke, left us to walk back.

I was convinced she had gone too far and left us with twenty yards more to walk than was necessary. I commented vociferously on this until Joan gave me a look that said 'stop wingeing' and we continued in silence. The terrain was changing dramatically now as we followed the coastline around the vertical cliffs of the muir of Ord. From that lofty headland the road drops steeply to the small fishing village of Helmsdale and as we descended the black blob became a little less black.

The fishing industry was established here in the last century by the Duchess of Sutherland in an attempt to provide alternative employment for crofters who had become displaced when their lands and houses were removed to make way for the more profitable land use of renting for sheep runs. This was during the tragic period of Scottish history known as the Clearances.

We reached Helmsdale and with twelve miles under the belt felt that we deserved a stop for refreshments. We made our way to a cafe we had discovered last year and gorged ourselves on the best doughnuts I have ever tasted.

Refreshed, we set off for Brora twelve miles away. It is on this stretch of road that a plaque commemorates the place where the last wolf in Sutherland was killed by the hunter, Polson, in 1700 AD. Obviously Greenpeace, Friends of the Earth, or the Hunt Saboteurs were not around then. Had they been the stone would have commemorated the spot where Polson the rat was hung, drawn and quartered for hunting creatures to extinction.

I was also approaching extinction. To allow my legs to recover from cramp I had reduced my intake of pills and potions that day. I was now being told I had not taken enough. I desperately fumbled for the medihaler as the familiar fire began to flare behind my eye. My hands were shaking as I squirted the drug-filled vapour down my throat. I staggered on. The pain got worse, reaching the point where further progress would become impossible. Joan, herself in pain from horrible blisters on her feet, looked on anxiously. The pain, though terrible in itself, did not get worse. I was able to stagger on and after forty minutes the pain started to recede as the drugs began to take effect. Exhausted legs were able to plod on.

As we approached Brora, the road skirting mile after mile of golden beaches, the wind arrow moderated to a slight ten miles per hour and the black blob melted with warm sunshine. As we strolled onto the camp site I met the warden.

'Not usually like this,' I said, referring to the blue sky and pleasantly warm sunshine.

To most people hurrying to finish at John o'Groats or hurrying to reach a more hospitable climate, Brora is a small fishing village that is only there to be passed through quickly. Few people notice the white surf and the golden sands of probably the most beautiful, unspoilt coastline in Britain. Fewer travellers still are probably aware of the existence of Capaldi's, manufacturers of award-winning ice cream with an international reputation.

For us that night Brora kept its most precious jewel hidden up a small street off the main A9. The Golden Fry fish restaurant is an unassuming place, selling fish and chips at unassuming prices. However, fish freshly caught that day, fried in mouthwatering crispy batter and with chips made from real potatoes, not frozen reconstituted stodge, ensure that the Golden Fry will always win my award for the best fish and chips in Britain.

It had taken us four days to get from Dunnet Head to Brora and in that time we had seen a change in the weather that now held reasonable promise. So far our route had been along the A9, hugging the coastline. For the next fifty miles three great firths carved into this coastline and our route would take us over the three mighty bridges that straddle them. Now, as I crunched my way through huge lumps of Brora batter, I thought about the next day when hopefully we would cross the first one, over the Dornoch Firth.

There is no way to train for walking marathon distances. The pounding the body takes cannot be prepared for by walking long distances with long rests in between, weight training, meditation or eating yoghurt-coated muesli for a month. The only effective training is to do it. It is the legs and feet that take the brunt and last year both Joan and I had to endure painful blisters. Joan in particular suffered intensely. By the time we reached John o'Groats we had become expert at lancing blisters, antiseptic techniques and elaborate wound coverings. This year we left armed with moleskin and zinc oxide plasters, needles of various sizes, scalpels, gallons of surgical spirit and enough cotton wool to run a nursery for a month. Joan's first blister appeared on her heel on the way from Dunnet Head. By Wick it had been added to and by the time we reached Brora she was collecing blisters on her toes. I was beginning to become concerned as to where it would all end but Joan was coping through the application of vast amounts of medication.

By now Andy and Zoe had established a routine between them. Zoe would normally ferry the lorry from one camp site to the next whilst Andy would take responsibility for towing the caravan. Taking daily turns, one would take responsibility for looking after the limping geriatrics, using the Discovery as a support vehicle whilst the other would look after home base, washing, cooking, exercising the menagerie, etc. It was during an exercise period that Andy had a problem with Rocky.

My son's dog, Rocky is sixty per cent fox terrier and forty per cent everything else. He was less than six months old when he came to us and we were his third home. He had been mistreated at both previous homes and what we got was a bewildered, nervous mutt. Rocky, however, has qualities, an eagerness to please, a bright, intelligent face, speed and agility and an abundance of charm being amongst the most endearing. Even Sherry, our irascible geriatric collie bitch, liked him. Only twelve months old, we could not face the thought of him being left on his own day after day whilst my son went to work so we had brought him with us.

Andy had taken the dogs for a walk in some woods when Rocky disappeared. Andy looked everywhere, searching in ever decreasing circles with ever increasing desperation. He was on the point of giving up when he spotted something moving in the undergrowth. Whatever it might be it was brown and stumpy. Closer inspection revealed a small white mound surrounding the quivering stump, two white branches stretching out either side. Even closer inspection revealed Rocky's tail, surrounded by Rocky's white bottom with Rocky's white rear legs either side. The rest of Rocky was subterranean. Pursuing a rabbit, he had followed his terrier's instincts and had followed the rabbit down its hole. A firm grip on the quivering buttocks, a hefty pull and a dirt-stained Rocky popped out of the hole like a cork out of a bottle.

The next morning, in promising sunshine, we set off for the Dornoch Firth. The lowest crossing point used to be at Bonar Bridge, made famous by a suspension bridge built originally by that great engineer, Thomas Telford. To get there the A9 followed a narrow, twisting road alongside the northern coast and then escaped by following a similar road on the southern side. A few years ago work started on a bridge much lower down the firth which promised to bypass twenty-eight miles of this torturous road. Originally planned to open in early 1990 the works soon ran into trouble and was rescheduled to open, first in late 1990 and then early 1991. Crossing over the new bridge was an important part of our plans so consequently we were horrified to discover that the grand opening had again been rescheduled, this time to 'Late Summer 1991'. Whilst the bridge was definitely closed to vehicular traffic we had received conflicting reports that pedestrians were allowed to cross. The risk of attempting to cross it seemed worthwhile. At worst we would walk a few wasted miles and risk prosecution for some vague infringement of trespass or bye laws. At best we would save twenty-eight horrible miles.

We approached the bridge.

'Ignorance is bliss,' said Joan, remarking on the absence of Keep Out signs.

As we skirted the first group of road workings, Joan's blissful smile became broader. Workers stared as we marched on, looking straight ahead like zombies wearing blissful smiles. At last we could see the end of the bridge. Our pace quickened. More workings loomed up. Then, from out of a hut stepped a man, BIG CHIEF written all over him. He came towards us.

'Pedestrians not allowed,' he said.

Joan smiled at him blissfully.

'You can't walk on the bridge,' said the man, walking

alongside us.

The end came nearer. We walked quicker. Joan engaged the man in ignorant coversation through clenched teeth.

'You can't walk in a hard-hat area,' puffed the man.

We walked even quicker. Joan smiled more blissfully. The man puffed deeper. We walked faster.

'No insurance . . .' gasped the man.

The end of the bridge was there. The man turned away. We were through. As we turned to look back from where we had come we were confronted by a big sign depicting a pedestrian axed in half by a red line and indicating KEEP OUT.

We were met by Andy a few miles further on and taken back to the camp site at Brora, to resume our walk the following morning in high spirits, probably influenced by the close proximity of the distillery responsible for producing a famous malt whisky. It was the end of day five and so far we had averaged nearly twenty-five miles a day. The awful weather at the start now seemed a long way away as we basked and walked in warm sunshine. That evening, as I enjoyed eating my way through Andy's culinary expertise, I pondered on the next day's walking.

The finger of land that separates the Dornoch and Cromarty Firth is famous for its holiday resorts, Invergordon being he most well known. The largest town, which would qualify for village status in England, is Alness, and that is where our next few miles of walking was to take us. From Alness the road then skirts the Cromarty Firth before crossing by means of another long bridge, this one over a mile and a half long. To finish the day the other side of the Cromarty Firth would entail a walk of over twenty-four miles and keep us ahead of schedule.

The next morning Andy dropped us off at our start point just the other side of the Dornoch Firth, before carrying on to the next camp site at Moy, fifty-one miles ahead and south of Inverness. Unable to use the bridge over the Dornoch Firth, Andy had to drive the long way round and we were able to appreciate what being able to use it meant to us.

In hazy sunshine we waved goodbye to Andy, the three dogs and contact with the world and set off for our first meeting point at Alness. This was the first opportunity we had to leave the busy traffic of the A9 and walk on some quiet secondary roads. The silence seemed eerie as the thunder of traffic died away and the only sounds to be heard in that still and misty air were the sounds of our own footsteps and breathing. Fairly soon the road became enclosed by the Glen Morangie forest and my thoughts drifted to the fine malt whisky of the same name. I heard the trickle of a stream and imagined water poured over ice. I heard the rattle of a stone my foot had kicked and imagined the rattle of ice in a glass. I imagined Joan sat in a deckchair and asking for an apple. What? Ask for an apple? I was broken out of my reverie by Joan asking again for an apple. Of course I had an apple. One of the penalties of walking off the beaten track this far north of Scotland is the sparsity of cafes, shops, pubs or any form of provisioning, so a day or half day's rations have to be carried. But why ask for an apple now, miles before our first planned break?

Then I saw it. Dobbin. Joan loves horses. Last year I lost count of how many equine friends she made. She talked more to horses than to me. I had no choice but to surrender a large green Granny Smith. Joan marched off with an apple, my apple, my lunch, and I was only a spectator as a grateful Dobbin indicated his appreciation by nodding his head up and down. Joan reached into her pocket for some peppermints. The nodding head nodded even more vigorously. Joan reached into her pocket for more sweets. The head threatened to become dismembered. Eventually, with Joan saying fond farewells to a bloated and farting horse, we set off again.

Fifteen miles after setting off we reached Alness, Joan looking forward to a cup of tea, me looking forward to buying an apple. As we were walking for a charity for disabled young people, we had some tee shirts and sweatshirts printed. These depicted the Star Centre logo of a girl in a wheelchair and a boy on crutches and we had surrounded this logo with the words Walking for Those who Cannot. The shirts were bright yellow and, with the logo, were extremely striking. As we walked through Alness people stared with what I perceived to be admiration. We heard a noise. It sounded like a Radio One roadshow. It got louder. People started to hurry off the pavement into shops, doors closed hurriedly with loud thuds. The noise got even louder. Then, from around a corner, hurtled a young man driving what appeared to be a turbo charged wheelchair and carrying a ghetto blaster playing at 120 decibels. The wheelchair carved a swathe through the crowded street, slow

pedestrians being bowled over. At the end of the street, Radio
One on wheels turned and came for another strafing run. What
I had originally perceived to be looks of admiration I now took
to be looks of hostility. I fumbled in the rucksack for our tracksuit
tops and having covered up our shirts we quit town.

From Alness we had a further four miles to go before reaching
the village of Evanton. Cramp was now affecting my legs quite
badly and I was in need of rest. Unable to see signs of souped-
up wheelchairs, Joan and I took a chance and popped into a
handy pub for lunch and refreshment. Feeling fresh and
restocked with apples we set off again and rejoined the A9 just
before the northern end of Cromarty Bridge.

Joan used to think that Cromarty was no more than a region
for shipping forecasts along with 'Dogger' and 'Irish Sea'. Now
she could see the firth that gives the shipping area its name,
and the graceful curve of the mile long bridge that crosses it.

In the opposite direction could be seen further examples of
twentieth century technology. Opposite Cromarty is Nigg Bay.
Sheltered waters, deep anchorages and easy access to the North
Sea made this a natural harbour for the fabrication of oil rigs
servicing the North Sea oil industry. In the distance we could
see some of these towering structures, looking lonely and forlorn
at their anchorages. Somehow the intrusion of the twentieth
century into this wild and isolated landscape looked strangely
out of place.

Just the other side of that bridge there is a car park and
hopefully Andy or Zoe would be there waiting to take us to the
camp site. The early haze had given way to warm sunshine and
I was becoming quite sunburnt. 'Better be careful,' I thought,
as we crossed the bridge to meet with Andy on the other side.
A few minutes later and we were on the southern side of the
mile long bridge and there was Andy. We finished the day with
another twenty-five miles under the belt, staying ahead of
schedule and apart from more blisters appearing on Joan's feet,
all was going well.

The next morning we were dropped of at our start point by
Zoe. The next few miles were again off the beaten track. It was
a Sunday which promised less traffic than usual, so we decided
to take Rocky and Sherry with us for the first ten miles,
arranging to meet Zoe the other side of the Moray Firth, near
Inverness.

Normally we would not take the dogs on our daily exertions as they can take up a lot of time but that day both Joan and I felt the need to take it slow, Joan because of blisters and me because of emerging sunburn. We were now on Black Isle, the strip of land bounded on the north by the Cromarty Firth and on the south by the Moray Firth. Black Isle is composed largely of rolling farmland with no major towns, the chief centres of habitation being Cromarty on the North Sea tip and Dingwall, where it joins mainland Scotland.

Rabbits abound in Scotland. Sherry, forgetting her eleven years and portly build, chased until she was exhausted. The rabbits thought that being chased by a fat, geriatric Border collie was hilarious and came back for more. Rocky was content to scrape up the flattened carcasses of the less swift rabbits unable to avoid recent traffic. We were enjoying warm sunshine. We came to the village of Munlochy and a welcome post office and general store where I was able to restock with apples, my original stock being donated to a succession of grateful nodding heads. Leaving Munlochy we soon joined the A9 again which, within a mile, took us to Kessock Bridge which crosses the Moray Firth. Shorter than Dornoch or Cromarty Bridges, Kessock makes up for its short length by a lofty height, towering above the village of North Kessock and offering a spectacular view over the Highland capital, Inverness.

Leaving Black Isle and a vast quantity of farting horses behind us, we soon met with Zoe in a handy lay-by. The weather was now getting hot. Bundling both dogs into the Discovery we bid farewell to Zoe and her canine passengers and began to walk the remaining ten miles to the camp site at Daviot and into Highland Scotland.

Highland Scotland

Shortly after leaving Zoe we left the A9 for a quieter road that ran parallel to it and which used to be the original road before a new, more level and straight dual carriageway was built. I soon found out why the road builders had followed a terrain-hugging curve rather than the straight line of the old road we were now puffing up. The road seemed to get steeper and steeper. The weather was getting hotter and hotter. My sunburn was getting more and more painful and Joan was hobbling on excruciatingly painful blisters. Fortunately we shortly came to a hotel and were able to enjoy a well-earned drink and a rest in the shade.

Sunburn was now a problem. Both Joan and I had suffered from windburn and Joan was on her third nose, the other two having peeled away long ago. My legs were now resembling lobsters and I was having to wear my waterproof trousers to keep the sun away. As we cooled off in the welcome shade of the lounge bar my legs started to burn with even greater ferocity. Kindhearted people looked on with sympathy as I plastered my legs with ice cubes and Joan tended to reddened and blistered feet.

'Never mind, not far to go now,' said one man, believing we were walking 'the right way round' and on our way to John o'Groats. We advised him of our reverse direction. The looks of sympathy turned first to pity and then to incredulity. The man turned away and talked to his friends about fishing.

Whilst I was burning and Joan's nose was peeling, Rocky was demonstrating his athleticism. On the camp site the rules were unyielding about dogs being on leads at all times. Rocky escaped from the lorry via a miniscule gap in an open window. Andy, mindful of the strict rules and fearful of being thrown off the site together with a mangled Rocky, searched high and low but Rocky could not be found. Outside a group of people were playing volleyball. Whilst looking for Rocky, Andy could not help but notice the site owner's dog was exempt from the strict rule and was in the middle of the group, athletically leaping up and heading the ball over the net. Presumably it must have been the site owner's dog as the owner was one of the group. Looks a bit like Rocky. IT IS ROCKY!

'Nice little chap,' said one of the group as Andy grabbed Rocky.

'Just came over to play,' said another one of the group as Andy desperately tried to get a lead round his neck.

'It's all right, he can stay with us,' said the site owner, forgetting his own strict rules. Rocky's charm had won the day.

We left the hotel and staggered further up the hill. A mile from the camp site and I was abandoning all plans for another twenty-five mile day. By the time we reached the camp site we had covered little over nineteen miles and I was grateful for that. I reached for the suntan cream. I was too late. As the evening wore on my legs began to burn with excruciating pain. It was difficult to believe that only a week ago we were shivering with cold. Whilst I was hopping up and down with sunburn, Joan was popping blisters and wallowing in surgical spirit. The lorry began to resemble a casualty clearing station. Andy came in to exercise his culinary skills. I was not in the mood for an exotic nut roast washed down with sparkling mineral water. A restaurant was attached to the camp site and that is where we made for, rump steak and chips washed down with cool pints of beer. As the beer began to anaesthetize my legs I started to feel better. I thought of progress so far and whilst today's total miles had been disappointing we had averaged an above schedule twenty-two miles to date. Tomorrow we hoped to reach Aviemore twenty-seven miles away.

We made a determined effort to get an early start for Aviemore. If the weather insisted on getting any hotter we would have to consider having a siesta in the afternoon, walking only in the cooler morning and evening air. I had suffered a night of disturbed sleep due to a number of attacks of neuralgia and I was now 'high' on pills. Joan's feet were getting worse. She now had blisters on every toe. On her left foot she had blisters between the toes. The blisters on her heels were not healing fast enough to prevent blisters forming under blisters. Each night they were taking an hour to treat and each morning an hour to prepare. The first hour of walking her face was a mask of pain and I was beginning to have great concern that she could continue. I looked forward to our first stop that would allow her some relief. I was also grateful for the effect the cool morning air was having on my sunburnt legs, which felt much better as they hid below layers of sunburn cream.

From the camp site we had the pleasure of a few miles of quiet road before reaching the A9, a mile from a small village called Tomatin. As we rounded each bend the highland scenery ahead grew more grand. Passing Loch Moy temptingly cool water sparkled in the early morning sunlight. Just past Loch Moy the road runs parallel with the A9 for a short distance before uniting at Tomatin.

There is a Little Chef café at Tomatin and I breakfasted on pancakes covered in maple syrup — the early morning air was obviously beneficial to both my sunburn and my appetite. Poor Joan was not only having to put up with a moaning lobster but one who ate pancakes for breakfast. The view from Tomatin whetted the appetite for what was to come. From west to east distant highlands rose proudly against a foreground of heather covered moor. There had been subtle changes around us too. The rolling green hills and forested lines of Black Isle had given way to high bare moorland.

The rest had eased the developing cramp in my legs and allowed weakened muscles to gather new strength. I was looking forward to the next part of the walk. Our route from Tomatin left the dual carriageways of the A9 and followed a lonely secondary road; what was the old A9, built before the modern dual carriageway came along with its flying leap over the Findhorn Valley. We came to the Findhorn Bridge with its striking high concrete parapet. Through the polygonal arches ornamentally let into the parapets, four generations of the civil engineer's art can be seen.

In the background is the modern road. Between the modern road and the old bridge stands the Victorian monument, a magnificent latticed steel structure carrying the railway to Inverness and beyond. Standing on the old bridge one can only marvel at the skills of Thomas Telford, whose original early nineteenth century bridge was not actually replaced until 1926. Telford himself borrowed his line from an even earlier veteran of highland road building, General George Wade who, in twenty years in the late eighteenth century, laid a network of roads throughout the Highlands where before none had existed. One can only marvel at the skill and fortitude of those early pioneers working with primitive tools in this harsh and desolate environment.

The Findhorn Valley has not only seen civil engineering changes. Successive dry summers and increasing water management projects have reduced what was once a mighty river to a tame ribbon of water. What was once a seething torrent is now a gentle, silvery sliver making its way to the North Sea at Burghhead Bay.

Shortly, old and new meet again and the modern A9 is rejoined just below Slochd summit. Since Inverness the road had steadily climbed to the summit, 1230 feet above sea level. This is a barren landscape, mile after mile of peat moorland broken only by outcrops of rock The Cairngorms, ever closer, now rise majestically to the south east and to the south and south west the Badenoch mountains could be seen.

After two miles of thunderous traffic we were able to rejoin the quiet and calm of the old road, illegally. Where old roads are not needed for access, the Highland Regional Council has practised a policy of fencing them off, making them inaccessible for pedestrians and vehicular traffic alike. Whilst I can understand the logic of not bearing the responsibility of maintaining roads no longer needed, is it too much to ask for a small gateway or other form of access to be placed in the barriers so that they can be used by the pedestrian? Why force pedestrians to mix with fast moving traffic on a major highway when a perfectly reasonable, traffic free alternative is available? Joan and I chose the alternative. Scrambling over a fence and round a rocky outcrop we were able to rejoin the old road. Our 'illegal' behaviour only lasted for a couple of miles before we joined with an unclassified road linking Slochd with Carrbridge.

I was looking forward to getting to the small village of Carrbridge and especially its visitor centre. It was getting warmer. I was becoming mindful of an incident last year when we were approaching the Strathclyde area in temperatures exceeding 85 degrees. As we approached Larkhall I was getting increasingly concerned about Joan, who was showing signs of heat exhaustion. We stumbled into Larkhall, desperate for a café. We found one. With immense relief we staggered in only to be told 'Sorry, half day.' Joan nearly collapsed. I started to look for taxis. As we staggered out a woman suggested we try the garden centre down the road.

Contemplating a nice cup of Weedol we staggered on. Half an hour later, stumbling over potted ferns, we emerged Tarzan-like into the garden centre café. 'We close in ten minutes,' said the woman. Then she looked at Joan who was near to collapse. 'All right, I'll make yee a cup of tea,' she said, 'but then I'll have to close as my husband get's angry when I'm late. 'Wheres yee come from?' she said as she brought the tea over.

We told her.

'Och, that's a long way in this heat' she said, 'you must have more tea.'

For the next hour that lady completely ignored the spectre of angry husbands and kept us continuously supplied with tea and ham rolls. Words cannot express our gratitude for the wonderful kindness she showed. The lesson of a year ago was not forgotten. I knew the visitor centre in Carrbridge contained an extensive café and restaurant and was looking forward to getting Joan there.

About three o'clock we arrived at the centre. The walk to Carrbridge had been outstandingly beautiful and the Cairngorms stood out grandly in the remarkably clear air. Even in late May their was still extensive snow at the higher altitudes and in the increasing heat and the ever increasing pain from my sunburnt legs the thought of taking a cable car ride and a roll in the snow nearly proved overwhelming. I made Joan sit in the shade and drink plenty of tea. I felt quite pleased about my foresight in recognising Joan's frailty to heat and was pleased I did not have to worry about myself. Suitably refreshed we continued our journey to Aviemore.

'There's someone skiing,' said Joan.

I was dreaming about rolling in the snow. Joan's words made me snap awake. All my fears about her fragility to heat came to life and I was concerned she was hallucinating. She repeated the words in perfectly lucid tones. My sunburn was hurting and I was in no mood for silly jokes.

'I'm being serious,' said Joan.

I was hot and irritable. I appreciated there was still snow on the Cairngorms but not enough to justify anyone skiing.

'Have a look,' said Joan insistently. I looked. I looked again, rubbing the sweat out of my eyes. In the distance I could see a skier. I was sure it was a skier because it was wearing a headband, goggles, a luminous stretchy suit and pounding along with ski poles. The only problem was that the skier was not enjoying what little snow was left on the Cairngorms but was in fact skiing down the A95 Grantown to Aviemore Road. I wondered about the tea we had been drinking. Perhaps the mushrooms we ate were the magic variety. The skier drew nearer as our two roads converged. I could now tell it was a lady. That explains it. She must be on a low flying broomstick. Finally the roads converged. Instead of skis the lady was attached to a skateboard on wheels. This convinced me that the female of the species must be totally incapable of coping with heat, going bananas at any increase in temperature.

Having convinced myself of male superiority in handling extreme climatic conditions we carried on walking whilst the lady carried on skiing to Aviemore. My sunburn was becoming extruciatingly painful and I was becoming extremely thirsty. One mile from Aviemore and I was beginning to stumble over my own feet whilst becoming ever more fretful about the searing pain from my legs. As we got into Aviemore I was finding it almost impossible to walk straight. Joan, showing no effects from the heat whatsoever, was becoming increasingly concerned about my condition.

We came into town. Joan ran to a chemist whilst I staggered across the road into a bar. As I sat there I started to shiver and voices became distant. A woman was talking to Joan. 'I'll get a blanket,' said a dismembered voice.

'Borrow my coat,' said another voice.

'I began to resemble a shelf at an Oxfam shop as the mound of clothing and blankets grew bigger. In Aviemore, as with all rural Highland areas, it is the police who are first on the scene to an emergency and it is they who orchestrate the other emergency services. They duly arrived. Having ascertained that the shivering pile of clothing and blankets was not suffering the effects of drink they called the emergency doctor, agreeing a rendezvous at a nearby health centre. Whilst waiting for the doctor they felt compelled to make their own contribution to the Oxfam collection and brought in a blanket which they placed on the only part of me left uncovered — my head.

The doctor duly signalled his arrival at the health centre and the two policemen helped me to my feet and assisted me to the police car. Thus the good people of Aviemore were treated to the spectacle of a balding middle-aged charity walker being escorted out of a bar by two policemen who covered his head with a blanket whilst leading him to a police car! On arrival at the doctor's I was helped out of the police car, still with the blanket around my head. Passing mothers shielded young children from the sight.

The doctor quickly determined I was running a high temperature but could find no obvious cause. He asked about any tablets I was taking and I gave him the extensive list. He consulted a book on pharmaceuticals and with a smile announced the possible cause. One of the large doses of drugs I was taking affect body metabolism and the way excess heat is disposed of. The bad news was that he instructed me to rest completely until my temperature had dropped to normal and not to walk in the sort of heat we have been experiencing.

Zoe arrived in the Land Rover and we returned to the camp site, having walked twenty-seven miles on a most eventful day. I was in sombre mood that night. I wondered how much we would be delayed by this health problem. We turned on the television and watched the weather man announce, grim-faced and with a hint of sadness, that the heat wave was about to come to an end. Cooler weather was on the way. Despair turned to disbelief, then to relief. Assuming I cooled down reasonably quickly, we might not be delayed that long. I thought about all the kindness I had been shown. My thanks to the people of Aviemore. Such care and kindness is a rare commodity but in Aviemore it was found in abundance.

For most of that night I was either shivering, drinking vast volumes of water or going walk-abouts to get rid of equally vast quantities of fluids that had reached the end of the plumbing system. As night turned into day I felt better, the vast fluid intake having a beneficial effect on body temperature if not on my bladder. We returned to Aviemore. In the hope that we might achieve some progress, Andy and Zoe moved camp to Newtonmore, nineteen miles further down the road. It was a sunny morning, so mindful of the doctor's advice we made an early start to get as much cool morning air as possible.

A few miles outside Aviemore on a quiet road is the hamlet

of Alvie and the beautiful little loch of the same name. Anyone looking at the sylvan setting, flanked by trees, a backdrop of heather-coated hills, must consider it a most tranquil place. Beauty can also be deadly. Closer inspection in the vicinity of Dulnain Bridge reveals a simple plaque of marble set in stone. Erected by local people, the plaque serves as a memorial to three young men who died on 26 April 1981 in a fishing accident. No one knows what happened. They were night fishing and were spotted at dawn, everything appearing normal. A little while later their overturned boat was spotted and the alarm raised. The waters in the loch are bitterly cold that time of year, being mostly fed by meltwater running off the mountains, and exposure to its icy grip would be deadly.

We reached Kingussie about lunchtime. After twelve miles of walking we were quite thirsty. Careful to drink plenty we went into the first place we saw, despite the somewhat scruffy exterior. Having had moderate quality refreshment, eaten in poor surroundings at rich prices, we then continued through Kingussie, passing café after splendid looking café.

Throughout our walk we always tried to carry a collection box with us. There were many acts of kindness. In Aviemore, whilst waiting for the police and the doctor, the kind people milling around to help placed whatever coins they had in the box. Many people in cafés and pubs gave us something. An incident occurred on the way to Newtonmore, three miles from Kingussie. Passing a petrol filling station we saw a woman tending the garden at the front. Noticing our box she asked us if we were walking. On our reply she immediately invited us into the shop and offered us anything we liked — ice cream, cold drinks, chocolate, etc. Whilst plying us with food and refreshment she put a large donation in the box and then as if that were not enough, took our box around her customers. Generosity such as this always popped up when most unexpected and was always a great motivator.

At Newtonmore we again joined the A9 and again found that the parallel old road had been fenced off by the Highland Regional Council. Choosing a policy of illegality similar to that at Slochd we bypassed the fence and enjoyed three miles of peaceful walking on a well-surfaced unused road to the camp site at Invertruim. Despite the events of the previous day we managed to walk twenty miles through bright, sunny weather.

The next morning was cool and misty. We left the camp site early and enjoyed two miles of peaceful walking on our 'illegal' road before rejoining the main A9. Our stay on the main road was a short one and in less than a mile we had left it in favour of an unclassified road that would take us to the small village of Dalwhinnie.

The previous year, arriving in Dalwhinnie, we met a man towing a horse and trailer up to John o'Groats where he proposed to ride the horse back to Land's End. Joan, passionately fond of horses, was concerned for the horse's welfare. Me, with painful blisters on my feet, thought as to where the man would get blisters and was concerned for his welfare. We later heard that Jim (the man) and Sue Ellen (the horse) successfully made it to Land's End.

There is not much in Dalwhinnie. It stands at the foot of Loch Ericht, which whilst being a large loch in the heart of the rugged Badenoch Mountains, is relatively plain and unscenic. It stands on the A869 which connects the A9 to the Spean Bridge — Kingussie road and could almost be called a short cut to Fort William. It boasts a couple of hotels, neither of which would sell us a bacon sandwich at ten o'clock in the morning. The most important thing in Dalwhinnie is a railway station and the consequent connection to Edinburgh and Inverness. As we were walking and not train spotting, this gave us no reason to hang about and we left Dalwhinnie fairly quickly, pondering as to whether Jim was able to sit down yet.

Rejoining the A9 we now climbed towards Drumochter summit. The A9 at this point follows Glen Garry which carves its way through the heart of the Badenoch mountains. Standing majestically in front of us was An Torc or the Boar of Badenoch as it is known in English. Whilst not being very high — most are less than three thousand feet, the Badenochs rise steeply from the surrounding hillside. Nearly all of them had patches of white snow, giving that extra touch of drama to the scene. As we climbed towards the summit the temperature gradually dropped, a welcome reprieve for my painful sunburn.

The summit of Drumochter stands at 1516 feet above sea level and is the highest point anywhere on the A9. It had been thirteen miles since leaving the camp site and we enjoyed welcome tea and cakes from a refreshment kiosk parked at the

summit car park. There was a further act of generosity when
we were told they were provided free as a donation for our
charity. As we drank our tea we were able to enjoy a grand vista
of proud mountains all around and to the west there were good
views towards Loch Garry. It is a classic highland scene.

From Drumochter summit the road drops gently towards Blair
Atholl and Pitlochry. Now a fast dual carriageway, we were
grateful to the road planners and builders for leaving a wide
cycleway at the edge. The weather was again warm, the cool
early morning mist giving way to strong sunshine. Again the
air was sparklingly clear and good views could be seen all
around. Leaving the old Boar of Badenoch behind, the old bore
and his wife made their way to their next change of road.

The scenery was again changing. High moorland and
grassland, gently rolling, was replacing barren lofty mountains.
All the locations here are 'lodges'. Dalnaspiedal Lodge,
Dalnarcardoch Lodge, etc. Anyone looking for an inn or an
hotel, however, would be disappointed. These are shooting
lodges, the surrounding moors being the home of grouse and
other game birds. On the east side of the dual carriageway there
is also a monument to General Wade known as the Wade Stone.
Erected in 1729 it marked the completion of a section of General
Wade's road that passed through Glen Garry and the Pass of
Drumochter. When the modern road builders arrived on the
scene they thoughtfully preserved this stone, moving it a few
feet to its current resting place. A simple plaque commemorates
the erection of this stone.

Four and a half miles from Drumochter summit an
unclassified road branches off the west side of the A9,
innocuously signposted Trinafour. It is in fact a very old road,
once the old A9 and previously one of General Wade's highland
roads. It also leads to some of the most outstanding highland
scenery that can be viewed from a road.

It's difficult to love a road. I fell in love with the A9. It is
the longest road in Britain, starting in Edinburgh and finishing
at John o' Groats. Following a north-westerly then an easterly
course, it bypasses Stirling before heading for Perth. A few miles
from Perth it bends again to go directly north to the very tip
of Britain. It is a fast road, not a concern to the walker, with
large stretches of dual carriageway and most bends being
straightened out. There are very few roadworks of the type that

plague English roads and there are nearly always wide verges for the walker or cyclist. Its architecture is impressive; it goes through some of the wildest and most beautiful scenery yet it never seems to intrude. Rather the opposite. For the walker it acts as a massive conduit for vehicular traffic leaving secondary roads blissfully quiet. As we left the A9 for Trinafour I could not help reflecting on the thought that apart from the occasional future glimpse we were now leaving behind a road that had been a constant companion for 230 miles.

The previous year we had avoided Trinafour. Camped at Loch Tay we experienced some of the worst weather we had to endure. The mist rolling off the hills was dense and any height above 500 feet would be cloaked in its clinging embrace. The thought of Iain taking the lorry over narrow roads edged with precipitous drops and climbing to a height of over 1200 feet was too much for my shattered nerves and we opted instead to do a circuit via Pitlochry and Blair Atholl.

The road to Trinafour is a narrow single track road that for the first three miles climbs 450 feet. As the road climbs the valley confines are left behind and an ever widening vista to the east and north-east opens up. Brown and purple heathery moorland, a backdrop of peaks, to the northeast the distant Cairngorms, glinting white and pink in the late afternoon sun. A distant line of electricity pylons draws nearer and the steep gradient starts to ease. A zigzag of bends, a rolling plateau and with startling suddenness the traveller is confronted with a vista of outstanding beauty. The road now drops suddenly down to Trinafour. Immediately to the right and 400 feet below lies Loch Errochty and its hydroelectric dam. To the left are the rolling plantations of Tummel Forest. The row of mountains shielding Loch Tay from the north, all of them Munros — i.e. peaks over 3000 feet, rear straight in front, dominated by the stark serrated outline of Schiehallion. As the road falls steeply downward towards Trinafour, glimpses of Loch Rannoch can be seen to the right. There is not much to Trinafour. A few houses and a heavily disguised hydroelectric power plant come first before the road meets the B847 from Blair Atholl to Loch Rannoch. As we followed this road towards Loch Rannoch we were treated to more outstanding views of the loch before we branched off left on another peacefully quiet, unclassified road to Loch Tummel.

The road climbed once more, Tummel Forest to the left,

before dropping steeply to Tummel Bridge. The drop seemed never ending and Joan suffered terribly as the angle of her feet caused the greatest pressure on those deep and painful blisters. I became gravely concerned and resigned myself to having to tell Joan at the end of the day that enough was enough myself; she had suffered enough pain and must now stop walking.

Where the River Tummel flows into Loch Tummel there are most pleasant riverside walks, picnic areas, loch and mountain views. On this warm and pleasant day we were met by Zoe with welcome refreshments of sandwiches and tea. In this tranquil setting, cloaked by trees and almost hidden from view, stands an enormous hydroelectric plant. The only indication to the casual traveller that something shocking was being generated were the columns of high voltage wires carried by pylons emerging abruptly from the trees and marching over the rolling hills to disappear into the distance.

From Tummel Bridge the road climbed steeply once more, through more forests, to a plateau at the delightfuly named Glengoulandie, before dropping to Coshieville and its welcome hotel. We briefly refreshed ourselves at the hotel before walking on and turning right onto a narrow unclassified road at Keltneyburn. The weather was warm and we were feeling fit, despite having surmounted three long, steep hills. Skirting round Comrie Castle, this pretty road winds its way to Kenmore in just over three miles.

Kenmore stands at the head of Loch Tay, giving some fine views over this beautiful stretch of water. When we camped here last year it was in miserable, cold weather. The rain poured down and for three days we did little else but stare at mist rolling down unseen hills. Today couldn't have been more different. Evening sunlight glinted on the still water. The enclosing hills threw down shadows and tall trees mottled the sunlight. We had to tear ourselves away. One more hill, the steepest yet, remained in our path.

Prior to tackling this steep hill I asked Zoe to take us into Aberfeldy, seven miles away, where I knew of an excellent café. I felt it necessary to broach the subject of Joan having to discontinue the walk and wished to do so in civilised comfort. Aberfeldy is a popular tourist spot and Joan needed to visit a chemist to stock up with yet more moleskin and zinc oxide. In the chemist's Joan entered into conversation with the assistant who was enquiring about her walk. Hearing of Joan's problem with blisters she brought over a tin of a newly introduced dressing specifically for blisters and recommended that Joan try them. We bought a couple of tins, doubtful that they would work but desperate to try anything.

The conversation I had with Joan in the coffee shop was a painful one. Her face was becoming permanently masked with pain. Even if she was able to endure pain that most people would find unbearable, I was concerned that infection or tissue breakdown would be inevitable and serious injury be the result. This walk meant as much to Joan as it did to me. On both trips we had covered an awful lot of miles together. Joan desperately wanted to continue and I could not bear to think of walking without my warm and humorous companion but facts had to be faced. It was a painful discussion. We both read the instructions with the new 'miracle cure' we had accidentally stumbled upon. Joan was optimistic, I was sceptical. Eventually we agreed that we would give the new dressings a try but if there was not a significant improvement over the next couple of days she would have to stop. With that gloomy thought we returned to Kenmore.

Continuing south from Kenmore an unclassified road climbs over 1200 feet to a moorland plateau before dropping equally steeply to Glen Quaiche and Loch Freuche. We wearily surmounted the hill and as the shadows lengthened dropped down to the small hamlet of Garrow at the head of Glen Quaiche. There we were met by Zoe and taken back to the camp site at Invertruim. It had been a memorable day. Twenty-five miles of steep ups and downs in perfect weather through glorious scenery. Tomorrow Andy and Zoe would move camp to Stirling whilst Joan and I intended walking from Garrow to the spa town of Crieff. For the rest of today we could enjoy the beautiful evening sky and mountain scenery.

The following morning Andy, towing the caravan, dropped us off on his way to Stirling. The road down Glen Quaiche is flat and uninspiring and the day was cool and overcast, a welcome relief to my now normal temperature and healing sunburn. Joan was walking painfully, although assuring me that the new miracle dressings were really having a favourable effect. We skirted Loch Freuche, then shortly before reaching the crossroads at Amulree we branched right on a footpath that led in two miles to the A822 Aberfeldy to Crieff road.

We found this track last year and half way along had been met by a large highland bull. Highland cattle have long, reddish hair and, more threateningly, huge, long slender horns. We came to an abrupt stop while Roger, as we christened him, stood there chewing the cud and staring dolefully through the hairy mane which fell over his eyes.

'You know all about bulls,' I said to Joan, referrring to the days ten years ago when she fed calves, 'you go first.'

Joan, reflecting on my courage, suggested instead that I should lead the way and have a man to man confrontation with Roger. I tentatively stepped forward. Roger blinked a doleful eye and I tentatively stepped back.

'I'm going down here,' said Joan, starting to round Roger from the right by going down hill.

'You'll get stuck in the mud,' said I, starting to round Roger from the left in an uphill direction. Roger dolefully stared straight ahead.

'You'll be going between him and his women,' said Joan retreating her muddy steps and referring to the cows further up the hill.

'Why don't you sing to him,' I said to Joan as I walked backwards downhill.

Roger's tail swished at a fly stupid enough to circle three tons of still breathing rump steak. He stared at the two wet humans in front of him. Highland cattle are supposed to be gentle creatures. Bulls are supposed to be passive when placed with cows. I wondered how many farmers had prematurely gone to the great slurry pit in the sky because the theory was wrong. The drizzle was turning to heavy rain. I thought of retracing my steps along two miles of muddy path but blanched at the thought of turning my back on Roger. Joan and I moved simultaneously, Joan choosing the low road and I choosing the high road. With quickening steps we regrouped a few yards behind his enormous rump. I screwed up my eyes, waiting for the enormous bellow, the shaking earth, the thunderous charge, the swish of those long horns. All I heard was my wheezing breath and pumping heart. I gingerly looked behind. Returning my stare was Roger, neck turned, dolefully reflecting on what shy, nervous creatures humans are.

This year the weather was warmer, if overcast. There was

no sign of Roger, only his cows. We reached the road and walked into Crieff. A short day in changeable weather. A pleasant day for Crieff is a pleasant town with many shops and cafés, a glass-blowing centre and a visitor centre. A telephone call to Andy arranging to be picked up later in the evening and Joan and I settled down to celebrating our arrival in one of our favourite small towns. An hour later Andy arrived and we made our way to the camp site at Stirling. Tomorrow a rest day in Stirling, the first rest day on the first day of June was planned.

Stirling is a beautiful city. It became the first capital of Scotland when, in 843 AD, an Irishman called Kenneth McAlpine (no relation to the chap who built large chunks of the A9), defeated the Picts in battle. As his tribe was called the Scots he quite reasonably called the country Scotland and plonked his castle on the imposing volcanic plug where Stirling Castle stands today. The castle dominated the fords of the Forth River, guarding access to the northern half of Scotland and, not surprisingly it was much fought over between the English and Scots. In 1296 it was captured by Edward the First but in 1298 severe retribution was handed out by William Wallace at the battle of Stirling Bridge and the castle eventually fell back into Scottish hands. In 1304 the castle was again seized by the English, led by Edward the First, but in 1314 the freehold was successfully contested by Edward Bruce, brother of King Robert.

The scene was now set for Scotland's most historic victory over the English. Edward the Second marched north with his army and the Scots, led by King Robert the Bruce, prepared to defend their kingdom. In fields by a small stream just outside Stirling the English were outwitted and outfought by the heroic Scots and routed. The battle was named after the stream, Bannockburn. Long after the nation's court was moved to Edinburgh, Stirling continued to find favour in Scottish hearts. Mary Queen of Scots was crowned in the castle and James the Sixth was baptised there. Today the castle stands in magnificent splendour overlooking the city.

We enjoyed our day off, wining and dining at excellent restaurants, enjoying Scottish hospitality. It was good for Joan's feet which for the first time showed signs of healing. Even with our day off, our average miles per day was fractionally over twenty-one, slightly better than schedule. I was also able to have a day off from taking pills. It was with relief that I allowed my

legs to recover from what was becoming a normal cramped state.
Weakened muscles restored their strength. As a special bonus,
despite the absence of a 'drug umbrella', the searing pain that
in varying degrees had afflicted me on every day since leaving
Wick was gratefully absent on this day.

Rocky also liked Stirling. Finding the tiniest gap in an open
lorry window, he managed to squeeze through. We had just
returned from Crieff and were surprised to find the usual excited
greeting from Rocky was absent. We all formed a search party.
We didn't have to look far. Rocky had just popped along to
see the neighbours, who were having a barbecue. When we
found him he was sitting demurely between the two of them,
admiring the man's culinary efforts.

We made our way over to apologise for the intrusion by our
four-legged friend.

'Nice little fella,' said the man, slicing the end off his steak
as his head disappeared in a plume of smoke.

Rocky's head tilted to one side, one ear pointing to ten o'clock
the other ear to five o'clock. Andy reached out to collect our
canine property.

'Pleasant little chap, just came over and sat with us,' said
the woman, cutting her steak in two and looking endearingly
at the pleasant little scrounging mutt who stared endearingly
back at her.

Rocky's head tilted the other way, ears flopping in the opposite
direction, tongue rolling slowly over drooling lips.

'He can stay a bit longer if he wants,' said the man, four foot
long barbecue tool in hand, reeling back from another plume
of smoke.

'We like dogs,' said the woman as Andy completely ruined
Rocky's evening by grasping his collar and hauling him away.

Refreshed from our day off we filled in the gap and walked
the twenty uninspiring miles between Crieff and Stirling.
Between those two towns is the small village of Braco. Last year,
travelling the other way, we had an exceptionally early start from
Stirling and reached Braco starving hungry at nine o'clock in
the morning. Joan tentatively popped into the local hotel to
enquire if they would serve us breakfast and we were pleasantly
surprised with a positive answer.

Tucking into bacon and eggs I remarked to the owner what
a fine collection of aeronautical paintings he had and as an

amateur pilot I was quite interested in that sort of thing.

'Yes,' he replied, 'whilst I own and work in the hotel, my main job is a commercial pilot with a well known airline!'

I looked at the waitress wondering whether to call her stewardess. I looked at our host, wondering if underneath his chef's hat there lurked a gold braided cap. I wondered about being on an aeroplane and being served breakfast by the pilot.

As we passed the hotel going the other way we remembered our flying breakfast with affection for it was the best news that day. The good news this day was that Joan was walking better and there were more signs of some blisters beginning to heal. I was still sceptical about the 'miracle dressings' but it was with more optimism that I thought about leaving the Highlands and looking forward to the next stage of our walk.

Just past Braco we reached the A9 and shortly left it to go through the town of Dunblane before reaching Stirling, the camp site and a large dinner prepared by Andy. It had been a short day but I was grateful. The pain had returned with a vengeance and I had taken significant quantities of drugs to keep it at bay. Now, as we approached Stirling, the familiar cramp spread down the calf muscle of my left leg. My feet began to feel numb and my walking was reduced to a painful hobble. The final two miles to the camp site took over an hour. To me it seemed like eternity.

Lowland Scotland

Joan and I left Stirling on 3 June to make our way to Strathclyde Country Park and into Lowland Scotland. The difference between the Highlands and the Lowlands has long been illustrated by an imaginary line drawn with its south-western edge touching the north of Glasgow, travelling north-east to a point near Braemar, then curving north to Inverness. By this definition Perth is Lowland country whilst Crieff is Highland country. Edinburgh is most definitely Lowland whilst Stirling is divided. Sometimes to the Scots as well there have definitely been two nations. Culloden was as much a Lowland versus Highland battle as it was England versus Scotland. Campbells massacred MacDonalds in Glencoe and Rob Roy, from his Loch Lomond base barely north of the highland line stole cattle from his lowland neighbours barely south of the line. Gaelic was spoken in the north whilst English was spoken in the south. Sassenach, a Gaelic word so often used in a derisory sense by Scotsmen to Englishmen does in fact mean Lowlander.

To Joan and I the only difference was the softening of the countryside and the increasing urbanisation. We were sorry to leave the Highlands for the people we had met there most definitely put the lie to the view widely held of the parsimonious Scot. Warmth, generosity and genuine friendship are to be found in great measure.

We left Stirling on pleasant little roads that followed the Auchenbowie Burn to Loch Coulter. Andy and Zoe were packing up when we left, moving camp to the delightful Strathclyde park. From the loch the road ascended at an easy gradient to Carron Bridge and its lonely hotel. From there the road climbs quite steeply, flanked by the Carron Valley forest on the west but with fine open views to the east overlooking the Forth Valley. About one and a half miles from Carron Bridge the road reaches its summit at the thousand foot contour before dropping steeply to Kilsyth.

I watched Joan's face anxiously on this steep downhill stretch. Her feet were hurting but thankfully the agonized expressions of a few days ago were absent. For the first time I began to have some confidence that a combination of a day's rest and new 'miracle' dressings might see us through. We descended gently into Kilsyth and with twelve miles on the score sheet and the weather reasonably warm we felt deserving of a drink and rest break.

Kilsyth is an old town, originally on a stagecoach route but now mostly in business as a dormer town of Glasgow. Some parts of Kilsyth are quite run down and we didn't hold out much hope of finding an Egon Ronay recommended cup of tea. The first café we went in wouldn't look astray on the set of a 'nuclear bomb goes off — people return to the dark ages' disaster movie. Groping our way through a thick fog of cigarette smoke, sliding on bits of grease that must have been accumulating on the floor since Bannockburn we eventually found ourselves at the rear of the establishment. I picked up a tray and a pool of cold tea slopped onto my shoes. I looked for a cleaner tray but realised I was holding the cleanest in the house. I asked for two teas and as I stretched to collect one a female gorilla collided with me from the rear and I was left holding half a saucer of tea and half a cup of fag ash. I looked at Joan who quickly got the message and we beat a hasty retreat, tea-stained trainers squeaking on the greasy floor.

We found another café and, not holding out much hope, we went in and found ourselves in an airy, spotlessly clean emporium of good food and service. The smiling waitress came up and, trying not to notice the tea stain on my shoes, took our order for bacon and egg sandwiches and a gallon pot of tea. In Joan's opinion she enjoyed the best bacon and egg sandwich she had ever had. Having refreshed ourselves and made a note of the café for future reference we got on our way and quickly returned into open countryside.

A few miles further, and we were approaching the concrete ramparts of two Greater Glasgow new towns, Cumbernauld and its smaller sister, Condorrat. Expanded rapidly in the sixties as one of the solutions to Glasgow's awful problems of slums and overcrowding, Cumbernauld contains all the worst excesses of planners with no greater vision than the bottom of a cement mixture. High rise flats and subterranean walkways, concrete playgrounds and plastic trees. How reminiscent of other new town districts, Hulme in Manchester, Basildon in Essex and the concrete cows and tarmac pastures of Milton Keynes, to name a few. Thinking of Milton Keynes made me grateful that the planners had stopped short of erecting concrete horses to accompany the concrete cows. Carting around concrete apples would be a real pain.

Conversely, Condorrat appears to suggest that the horrendous mistakes of the sixties have been lessons painfully learnt. Lower rise housing, real grass and bushes, shops that don't rip you off because they're the only ones for miles around; perhaps there is hope yet.

As we approached this new town I studdied my map with intensity. My mind went back to last year as we approached from the south. It was the 3 May. We were at Cumbernauld. Complementing myself on the excellence of my map reading, I had carefully navigated our way street by street through Condorrat. Gradually the picture around me became different to the picture suggested on the map. As we passed the same telephone box for the third time that day a feeling of silent panic welled up in my throat. Resisting the temptation to show weakness by asking someone where we were, I tried variation 4D that I had planned. First left, second right, through the underpass, then up the steps to the roundabout. As I stepped triumphantly out of the underpass I felt like a gladiator stepping into the arena for the first time. We were standing in the middle of an intersection of immense proportions. I looked in terror around me. Joan was looking at a Glasgow Corporation bus. I read the road signs — M74, A80, M80, M9, Perth, Stirling, Glasgow, Leningrad, Vladivostock. Joan had that look on her face that said, 'What now, clever dick?' I looked at the maelstrom. I looked at Joan. I looked at the bus. We returned to the camp site ignominiously ferried by Glasgow Corporation Transport. The following day we bypassed this pedestrian no-go area by a more circuitous route.

This year I hoped we had got it right. Down a road past a sign that said Dead End, along a footpath, T-junction, turn left, mini-roundabout exit, at two o'clock, all was going well.

Footbridge over a tarmac canyon, neat little houses, rows of bushes, footpath separating people from traffic in a delightfully rural way; the planners had learnt something, we were in Condorrat. Half a mile of footpaths, a small road — turn left, right after 400 yards, we were in open country. I breathed a huge sigh of relief. Clear round, no faults. Wagner's Ride of the Valkyries echoed in my head as I strode triumphantly past a farm whose sign indicated we were on the right road. Joan gave me a My Hero look and wondered whether the stain from the cow pat I had just trodden in would match the tea stains, now fading to a delicate shade of light tan.

Four more miles of rural farmland and we were in Coatbridge. Three miles of downtown streets and we were in the amazing green jewel of Strathclyde Country Park. Thirty-one miles of walking had seen us leave Stirling and cross the Greater Glasgow area with only three miles of tramping streets. By the time I reached the pub that night the symphony in my head was playing Hail the Conquering Hero. Joan was also cautiously celebrating. The new dressings we both held hope for were working and her feet were mending. We were both becoming optimistic that this awful, painful problem was beginning to come under control.

Strathclyde Country Park is a towering monument to those far-sighted visionaries who first conceived it, planned it, designed it and built it. It lies at the heart of the greatest urban sprawl in Scotland with Bothwell and Greater Glasgow to the north, Bellshill to the east, Motherwell to the south-east and Hamilton to the south and west. To the west it is flanked by the M74 motorway with connecting junctions at its southern and northern extremities. Measuring about three square miles it is rolling grassland interspersed by paths and recreational tracks. At its heart is Strathclyde Loch, providing bathing beaches and water sport facilities. At its northern end, just off the motorway intersection, is a camp site that ranks as one of the best in Britain. Plentiful, modern facilities and a thoughtful layout ensuring privacy for each unit ensure that Strathclyde Country Park will always feature in my top ten list of camp sites.

Seeing Strathclyde Loch again reminded me of a potentially disastrous incident the previous year. In broiling hot weather we had returned to the site from Cumbernauld. Joan looked at the bare patch of earth where once had stood our lorry.

'He's probably gone swimming in the Loch with Sherry,' said

I, feeling rather stupid.

We sat down and waited, already feeling depressed from having to retreat in the face of overwhelming odds in Cumbernauld. An hour went past, no Iain. The site warden made us a cup of tea. People started giving us odd stares, wondering what we were doing there without a caravan. Another hour went past. The sun was beginning to set. The site warden contacted the park warden's office and they agreed to hold a search of the park if Iain did not reappear in another hour. Another hour, another cup of tea and still no Iain. The sun slipped down the horizon by another few degrees. Joan was becoming frantic. I was beginning to wonder what people's reaction would be when confronted by two people with no home, no clothes, no money, dressed only in tee-shirt and shorts and telling an improbable story about walking from Land's End to John o'Groats.

The site warden was taking details of what Iain, Sherry and the lorry looked like when, from out of the gathering gloom, Iain appeared, trailing a wet and bedraggled Sherry behind him.

'Where have you been?' I asked, not daring to ask the $64,000 question about the whereabouts of the lorry.

'Swimming in the loch,' said Iain sombrely. Sherry's canine sixth sense told her to hide. Joan waited. I prayed. Sherry chased a cat and nobody cared. Iain, head bowed, stood there dripping with water, summoning up courage to finish the story. Then he said it.

'I've lost the keys,' he said. One complete set of lorry keys were at the bottom of Strathclyde Loch!

I stared numbly at the dripping youth in front of me. What could have been a classically disastrous attack of Murphy's law was about to be narrowly averted by one of those strokes of good fortune that sometimes strike the afflicted. I always carried a spare set of keys in the rucksack. That morning, because of the heat, I chose to leave it behind. On the way out I hesitated, feeling rather naked, and asked Joan if there was anything in the rucksack she needed.

'No,' she said, 'but take the keys just in case.'

The case now stood in front of me. I jangled the keys six inches from a dripping nose and asked Iain to take us to the lorry. There was no point searching further. Iain, in mounting panic, had spent the last few hours doing nothing else.

Now, as we breathed in the early morning air, we thought of Iain just over a year ago. A young man just turned nineteen, facing a desperate situation with no one to turn to, no one to console him, no one to share the burden with. At the time I was too overcome with relief at seeing him safe and sound and too angry at a lost set of keys to give his inner emotions much thought. My heart on this beautiful June morning was now with him.

Sherry liked Strathclyde Park. Up till now she had enjoyed her relationships with Andy and Zoe, who would spend many hours excercising the dogs. She had no wish to be with us. She had had enough of that last year, being dragged from one end of the country to another. Shortly before we left I took her for an early morning constitutional and, reaching a patch of rough ground, let her off her lead; no problem with an intelligent, well-trained sheepdog like Sherry who obeys every command. In Sherry's life there are two lifeforms lower than anything else. One is cats, the other is joggers. There were no cats stupid enough to be out that early, only joggers. Hundreds of them. Emerging from behind every bush, round every bend. Before I realised my mistake Sherry was off, deaf to commands from her desperate owner. The next few minutes were bedlam as jogger after jogger was made to perform like a four minute miler. Fortunately she was stuck for choice. Realising there was no real sport involved and feeling her advancing years, she made her way back to the lorry, leaving one red-faced, panting charity walker to apologise to half a dozen extremely breathless joggers whose half mile jogs had been extended by a factor of five.

Leaving Sherry with my wrath still echoing in her ears we set off for the small town of Douglas twenty-four miles away. From the camp site we rounded Strathclyde Loch and, crossing under the motorway, left the park at its south-western extremity. A couple of urban miles further on we were passing the garden centre which was the scene of so much kindness a year ago. Nothing ever stays the same. It was a different woman and the tea was dreadful. A few more miles and Larkhall was behind us.

Joan and I have spent many holidays in Scotland and have great respect for Scottish business instincts. Throughout the world emigré Scots have founded great industries. The great Scottish tartan is one example of exploitation of a natural resource.

Scottish tartans are famous throughout the world and from all corners of the globe there are people queuing up to prove Scottish heritage, to have the right to wear a Scottish tartan, to belong to tartan societies. Anyone visiting Scotland can only be impressed by the success of this multi-billion pound industry. Souvenir shops, crammed with foreign visitors, sell tartan momentos by the thousand. Run down old buildings are sold off for millions as 'ancestral' homes. A look at the lists of clans and names that can be associated with them will convince anyone that they enjoy Scottish heritage.

For the most part it is a fake! The plaid, the tartan kilt was originally the dress of the highland clansman. In that harsh, barren landscape the folds of cloth not only provided the dress but also the bed, the cloth being wound round the body at night to keep the elements at bay in that shelterless environment. Often the plaid would be soaked first, matting the fibres together and providing for a more windproof cover. To identify his clan, the Highlander would often colour the plaid with natural dyes from local soils and berries.

The wearing of the tartan was popularized by Queen Victoria when in 1848 she acquired Balmoral Castle. It was a Scottish barrister, John Camden Neild, who bequeathed Victoria the money to build the new castle, one of the principle architects being her German husband, Prince Albert. The Queen had it decorated from top to bottom in plaids and Prince Albert even designed a tartan exclusively for the Royal Family. The Queen regularly attended the Highland Games at Braemar, always clad in a variety of tartans.

It was this royal patronage that popularized the wearing of tartan that has been so skillfully exploited ever since. Clan societies sprang up like wildfire in the Victorian era and the 'rules' relating to the wearing of a tartan became formalised. Jackets to go with the kilt were invented, the carrying of pistols — never the armament of a Highlander — became mandatory, the carrying of a shepherd's crook became obligatory for walking, despite the fact it was the sheep that displaced so many Highlanders from their homes, and ultimately, their country.

During our walk through highland country I could not help but think of the great fakes and fakers. John and Charles Stuart, purportedly descended from the Young Pretender, produced coloured drawings of over fifty tartans which were all successful fakes! Ronald McIan, who published the books *Clans of Scottish Highlands* and *Gaelic Gatherings* was another highly successful faker. If they could do it, why couldn't we? After all if a German could invent a Scottish tartan then surely the whole thing is up for grabs! For many miles Joan and I discussed the commercial merits of becoming fake clan chiefs.

We thought of a name, McBogus, (pronounced Boggus) and the two branches of the clan that settled in England and Wales, the Smiths and the Jones. We constructed the sad cycle of forced emigration to the New World and to the Far East, Smith being pronounced Mishi, Boggus changing to Bishi, and Jones changing to Joshi. We then thought of the marketing, where anyone in the New World or the Far East whose names were Smith or Jones, or end in Bishi, Mishi, or Joshi, could for a small fee register as a clan member. We thought of erecting a 'Wimpey' built castle on every new housing estate on the grounds that there would be at least fifty people whose names were Smith, Jones, or end in Mishi, Bishi, or Joshi. We thought of a tartan in revolutionary stripes, coloured with environmentally friendly greens, browns, and blacks.

We then walked into Kirkmuirhill, ten miles from Larkhall. It was Bin Day or waste collection day. Hard working people were emptying bins, extracting waste-filled polythene bags and replacing them with fresh ones hanging from their waist. They wore black jackets supplied by the corporation. From their waists swung polythene bags, green, black and brown ones forming a striped kilt. The McBogus Tartan had come to life! We cracked up. Helpless with laughter we reeled all over the road as startled pedestrians hurried by, giving a wide berth to the two jabbering lunatics laughing hysterically over nothing.

The next two hours' walking was painfully slow due to the need every five minutes to collapse into a giggling heap. We thought of the marketing potential of a polythene kilt, polythene castles and a polythene sporran that doubles as a supermarket carrier bag. Slowly sanity returned and we continued walking with a bit more purpose and a bit less sanity.

Joan was walking better, the miracle plasters working miracles. Eventually our route took us on to what used to be a section of the A74 trunk road between Glasgow and Carlisle, recently bypassed by a new section of the M74.

'I'll be a happy man when we reach Carlisle,' I shouted to

Joan who was one hundred yards away on the other side of the road. Joan was reflecting on Scottish methods of road improvement. No digging up the old road, no contraflows, no diversions. They just build a new road alongside the old. We were walking on a road which consisted of four carriageways, two footpaths and a central reservation.

'They throw away better roads than we keep in England,' shouted Joan as the third car in two hours passed us. A few more miles we came to a transport café. We had walked considerably further than planned due to constantly having to cross the super highway to talk to each other.

Having refreshed ourselves with bacon sandwiches and superb tea we marched on. Soon we came to the end of our desolate highway and turned off onto the Douglas road. A few more yards and we were able to turn off this road and onto a bridle track through Douglas Park, part of the estate belonging to Douglas Castle, a ruin in much need of repair. It was cool and cloudy. The weather forecast spoke of a forty per cent risk of showers and they were right. Showers often threatened but never quite materialised.

The track followed the banks of Douglas Water, a pleasant little river, and Joan and I enjoyed the solitude of the weekday evening. It had been twenty miles since leaving camp and in a couple more miles we were due to be met by Andy in Douglas. Andy would take us back to the camp site at Strathclyde Park for the last time, as we planned to move camp to Sanqhar the following day.

We were getting well practiced at meeting each other. Normally Joan and I rang from a public call box to the mobile telephone carried in the Discovery or lorry and gave details of time and place. Where we knew communication was going to be difficult we either arranged to meet at a pre-determined place and time or Andy or Zoe would keep with us, meeting every few miles en route. It was very important for Joan and I to have this lifeline of contact. Very often we were travelling light, little money, little clothes, little idea of what we were doing and very often on little roads difficult to follow in a car. Today things went without a hitch. We duly arrived at Douglas and Andy, dead on time, was there to meet us at the prearranged spot.

The next day Andy dropped us off before going on to Sanqhar and we resumed our walk. A couple of miles of walking along the Kilmarnock road and we were able to turn off onto an unclassified road heading into the Lowther hills, part of a network of hills that are collectively known as the Southern Uplands. The road started to climb steeply and soon we were rewarded with fine views to the north, although a haze was beginning to form. The scenery here is much softer than that of the Highlands, hills roll rather than soar, grass rather than heather is the usual covering. The road, making wide sweeps around prominent tops, is unfenced and the feeling of fresh open space after the confines of Strathclyde urbanisation was almost intoxicating.

After six miles we joined the Crawick Valley road running between Lanark to the north-east and the village of Sanqhar to the south-west. This road is breathtakingly beautiful and despite linking Sanqhar to the A74 is peacefully quiet. Twelve more miles and we reached Sanqhar. Lying in Nithsdale with its back to the Southern Uplands, this delightful village is an important staging post for the hardy walkers traversing the Southern Uplands way, the long distance path that connects west coast with east coast. Two hundred and twelve miles long this long distance path was Britain's first coast to coast way starting west of Stranraer and finishing just south of Dunbar.

The camp site for the day was the grounds to the rear of the Blackaddie Hotel. It is a certificated location of the Caravan Club. Put into English, the Caravan Club, following strict guidelines, is empowered to certify certain locations to allow camping. The club has a directory of over 4000 such locations, the minimum standards being a supply of drinking water and a disposal point for the contents of chemical toilets. There can be no more than five units on site at any one time. In exchange for privacy and often unique and relaxed surroundings, the happy camper often has to put up with only the minimum facilities. Not so with the Blackaddie Hotel. First surprise is the provision of electrical hook-ups. Second surprise is the provision of shower and bathroom. Third surprise is the pleasantness of the hotel facilities — fine food, fine beer and fine hosts. We enjoyed our stay at the Blackaddie Hotel!

It was late afternoon when we arrived and we already had twenty miles under the belt. Having refreshed ourselves with large quantities of Zoe's tea we decided to do another six miles. Andy was talking to other campers on the site, some visitors from Holland, as we outlined our objectives and the picking up point. Our route now was to follow unclassified roads along the south- west bank of the river Nith, throught the delightful Eliock woods to the classic stone Bridge at Glenearlie. As it was a short walk in warm evening sunshine along a very quiet road we opted to take Sherry and Rocky with us.

The area teemed with rabbits. Sherry, feeling athletic, decided to chase one and set off with a thundering stride. The rabbit looked up and seeing what it was being chased by casually strolled away. Rocky was about twenty yards behind us, trying to scrape the carcass of a dead rabbit off the floor. He looked up with a bored half eye to see what the geriatric hound was getting excited about. Seeing the rabbit strolling away he was overcome with family pride and decided to intervene. Half a second later we were overtaken by a tan and white blur. The rabbit, seeing the threat, pressed turbo boost. A quarter second later Rocky overtook the puffing Sherry. The rabbit went faster. Rocky, ears pinned back, hind legs overtaking front legs like a whippet, was gaining rapidly. The rabbit went faster. Not fast enough. Three, four, five strides, a flying leap and ...

'ROCK-EEEE!' Both Joan and I yelled simultaneously. Rocky hovered in mid-air. His brain worked overtime. Had he earned enough Brownie points this week to risk disobedience? Had he done enough to satisfy family honour? Did he really like rabbit stew that much? Decision made, all four legs were spreadeagled and he crashed to the ground, letting the doomed rabbit escape down a hole. He came swaggering back, shoulders rolling, tail wagging, a look on his face that seemed to say, 'That showed 'em!'

We reached Glenearlie Bridge at the prearranged time and waited for Andy. Half an hour later we still waited for Andy. An hour later, with mounting alarm, we were still waiting for Andy. The dogs were restless and it was getting dark. We were six miles from civilisation, no phone box and only the occasional farmhouse anywhere around. A further half hour went by and I now made the decision to walk back to Sanqhar along the main road. By this time we had convinced ourselves that Andy, always punctual, always conscientious, must have had an accident. At least if I got back to Sanqhar I could return in the lorry.

It was with great apprehension that I left Joan alone in that isolated spot. She was very tired but I still felt fit enough to jog or run back so it was better she stayed rather than walk six slow miles back. She had the two dogs to protect her and Sherry in particular could be a fearsome adversary. I started to run and at the same time frantically wave a thumb at passing traffic. The miles rolled on. With each passing minute I became more frantic. My feet were sore, my legs tired but the urgency to get to civilisation and come back to relieve Joan was overwhelming.

It was now very gloomy twilight. I heard a car and fortuitously stopped and looked behind. It was being driven straight at me. With horror I dived backwards into a thorny hedge as the car wheels scuffed the edge of the road, sending up a pile of dust where two seconds previously I had been standing. I was quite shaken and as I watched the car lights disappear into the distance I reflected on the sort of drunken or half asleep idiot that must have been at the wheel. It did not occur to me that it was anything but a clumsy accident.

Any thoughts I had that it was accidental were dispelled when shortly the same car went past in the opposite direction, turned and came back again. With mixed feelings of disbelief and terror I now realised that in this isolated part of Scotland someone was deliberately trying to run me over. I was being attacked by a maniac who wanted to add a bit of homicide to his career. I do not know why. For the second time I dived into prickly thorn bushes and for the second time I felt the waft of warm air as steel and rubber missed my legs by inches. The car sped off again in a cloud of roadside dust. I was now extremely shaken. I again heard the sound of a car behind me and almost dared not to look back. I did. With huge relief I recognised our Discovery, Andy at the wheel, Joan beside him. I could have wept with joy and relief but instead climbed into the back seat displaying temper and emotion I was later ashamed of.

What had happened to delay Andy was a series of incidents that, had they been isolated, would have been harmless, but which together made a dangerous chain reaction. We were in a hurry to leave the camp that night, wanting to enjoy the evening sunshine. Andy was talking to the Dutch visitors and was distracted when I gave him the rendezvous instructions. There are a series of bridges that cross the river Nith, linking our road to the main Kilmarnock road and we were going to the second one. When Andy set off to meet us he used the main road, found the bridge and waited until we were overdue.

Normally this would have alerted him that something was wrong but on this occasion, unusually, we had the dogs with us and that gave good explanation for the delay. Having his own dog, Ben with him he thought it a good idea to take Ben for a walk. Crossing the bridge he took our unclassified road back towards Sanqhar, hoping to meet us en route. Because he arrived by a different road he did not know that we were not between him and Sanqhar. Fifteen minutes later he realised that something was wrong and spent another fifteen minutes walking back to the Discovery. He did the right thing by driving back to the camp site because in normal circumstances we would have contacted the lorry, but on this occasion we were miles from a phone box. Finally realising he had been to the wrong bridge he carefully retraced our route, eventually finding Joan an hour and a half after the prearranged time.

The root cause was complacency. Up until now all our rendezvous had been on main roads or in prominent places. We had become used to the support team always being able to find us and they had become used to finding us with little problem. Complacency was fortuitously discovered on a day when it was dry and warm and Joan could be left alone with two dogs to protect her. Safe back at the Blackaddie Hotel, we analysed events. We all had a part in what went wrong. Sober and with complacency firmly put on the shelf we went to bed.

The next day we set off hoping to reach the small village of Duncow, six miles from Dumfries and on the way to Lochmaben and Gretna Green. The previous evening I had deliberated reporting the incident with the maniacal motorist to the police but now it seemed an awful long time ago, a bad dream, something best forgotten. We were dropped off by Andy at the right bridge and, leaving him and Zoe to move camp twenty miles down the road to Penpont, we set off.

The weather was bright and sunny and we were looking forward to the walk through the heart of Nithsdale via Drumlanrig Park with its pink fairy-tale castle. An outstanding walk, the roads are narrow, virtually deserted and offering fine views across the valley to the rolling contours of the Southern Uplands. All around is rolling parkland offering picnic spots every few yards. The river Nith, clear and cool, flanked by green meadow, provides the jewel in the centre of this enchanting landscape. Even the haze that had been building up all morning could not spoil the panorama that unfolded as we first climbed out of the confines of Eliock wood, strode along a crest of a ridge, and then dipped down to the banks of the Nith.

We stopped at the river bank for a picnic. I laid out the pies and orange juice and Joan bathed her sore but healing feet in the pure cold water of that delightful river. I searched for our apples but remembered the sight of two nodding heads two miles back. This was an idyllic situation and it was with reluctance we packed up to leave a short while later.

After twelve miles of this sustained beauty we arrived at the small crossroads of Thornhill. A pleasant town, we found an excellent café in the baker's. Getting up to go we were told, 'As you are walking for charity there is no charge'.

It was not only the weather that was warm, as so often we found Scottish hearts to be that way. Refreshed, we set off to resume our acquaintance with the Nith. Four more miles of beautiful scenery and we eventually left Nithsdale at the hamlet of Auldgirth to head for Lochmaben in a north-easterly, then south-easterly curve. At six o' clock we met Andy without any difficulty. We wanted to walk further but felt the need for everything to be right after the day before. Complacency had been completely swept out of the window and we had a number of contingency plans available should things go wrong, but it was nice to have everything go like clockwork.

We arrived at Auldgirth on 6 June. Joan's birthday was on 8 June.

'What a birthday present for Joan,' I thought, 'if we could walk into England on her birthday'.

I looked at the map. We would really have to finish close to Gretna Green by tomorrow night if we were to be sure of walking into England at a leisurely pace the day after. On the route we had planned Gretna Green was thirty-five miles away. Joan's feet were still sore but blisters were now healing faster than they were forming. We were both feeling fit. Thirty-five miles was not an impossible task even if the terrain was rather hilly.

Andy dropped us off at Auldgirth and disappeared in the direction of Carlisle. The Land Rover was in need of a service and the nearest agents were in that English border town. For the first time on the walk we knew we were completely without backup support until Andy returned in a loan vehicle. We had agreed to meet again in the vicinity of Lochmaben and it was in that direction that we now headed.

From Auldgirth we left the River Nith behind us and set off along a small secondary road towards the village of Duncow. Today the road was fortunately quiet, a pleasant change to the previous year. Then it had been a Saturday. A little further up the road there had been a motor sport event which had just finished and the spectators were using this little road as a short cut home. For three miles Joan and I had walked in fear of our lives, plastered firmly into the hedgerows as one budding Nigel Mansell after another roared past us.

'Nearly quarter of the way there,' I said, as Joan surveyed the scene in front of her, a boulder strewn footpath climbing steeply to a crest of a ridge. We were eight miles from Duncow and on a footpath taking us to East Tinwald and then on to Lochmaben. June 7 had just dawned grey and cool. Rain was threatening but never quite arriving. I sat on a moss-covered boulder, enjoying our first break of the day, a revolting saccharin-sweetened blackcurrant drink and a three-day-old pasty. A steep climb up, a steep descent down and we would reach the flatter and better surface of the A709. We marched on. Joan's feet did not like the downhill bit, especially the frequent banging of toes against rocks, and I began to get the impression that reaching England on her birthday was no big deal to her.

We reached Lochmaben and found an uninspiring café overlooked by a statue to Robert the Bruce who once had a cave nearby before exchanging it for the more salubrious accommodation of Stirling Castle.

'A third of the way there already already,' I said enthusiastically to Joan, who groaned and went to talk to a horse.

A short distance out of Lochmaben and we were able to leave the busy road that goes on to Locherbie for quiet lanes taking us towards Ecclefechan and ever nearer to Gretna Green. We were met by Andy who having taken the Land Rover into Carlisle for servicing, had returned in a borrowed Austin Montego. Andy offered us sandwiches and a flask of tea before heading off eight miles down the road to the next rendezvous. Joan looked a bit tired but an emerging sun was cheering us up.

'Not far now,' I said, as Joan's face brightened, 'to the half way point,' as she threateningly picked up a rock.

A few more miles and we were on a footpath crossing a steep

hill to Bonshaw.

'Those cooling towers must be in England,' I said enthusiastically to Joan, pointing to some tiny specks on the horizon. Joan wearily groaned and muttered something like, 'How much longer?'

'Just one more effort and we'll be in Gretna,' I said cheerfully.

What goes up must come down and with dragging feet Joan was soon painfully descending another boulder-strewn path. She wearily plodded on.

'Been a nice day,' I said intelligently, trying to cheer Joan up. 'If this sort of weather lasts we could probably do the same distance again tomorrow and be well past Carlisle.' Joan spotted another horse and deserted the jabbering idiot at her side in favour of an intelligent conversation.

One mile from Gretna Green we were met by Andy.

'You can do it,' he said enthusiastically to a sleepwalking Joan. Her unprintable reply indicated she wanted a lift. Exhausted we returned to the camp site. That night I looked at the map. One mile into Gretna Green, a few miles towards Longtown and into England on her birthday.

'Been a real effort today,' I said to Joan, 'but I really don't mind putting the effort in if it gives you a really nice birthday.'

Joan was sharpening the carving knife.

The following day we reached Gretna Green and popped into a café for breakfast. I tucked into a huge pile of eggs, bacon and fried bread whilst Joan had a short sleep. Leaving Gretna Green Joan popped into the old blacksmith's shop, scene of so many quickie marriages until sixty years ago, to see if they do quickie divorces as well. Leaving disappointed she spotted a horse to give my apple to.

Two miles later and we were standing against a sign that said Cumbria.

'Happy Birthday,' I said to a slumbering Joan.

A few minutes after leaving Scotland and it began to rain. 'Ironic,' I thought, 'all the way through Scotland with just a few showers and no real rain, get to England and it rains!'

'Can't last long,' I said to Joan as the refreshing rain threatened to wake her up. As forecasts go, these words must stand alongside those of the captain of the *Titanic* as he turned and said, 'What icebergs?'

Preparing for departure from Lands End.

Snow in Somerset! This is on top of the Blackdown Hills.

Ascending Shap. The long and winding road! Although nowhere particularly steep, it is a long and continuous ascent.

Towards Drumochter summit on the ''New A9''.

The new bridge at Loch Tay.

The Gretna Green to Longtown road taken with auto timer!

The Eden footbridge to Sedgewick, outside Kendal.
A really beautiful campsite couldn't quite overcome the
depressive effects of the weather.

The "A" team at Jamaica Inn.

Northern England

The road from the Scottish border to the crossroads town of
Longtown and the junction with the A7 Carlisle to Edinburgh
road has few attractions and we were pleased to get the necessary
three miles behind us and find a café that sold strong black coffee.
We had chosen to come this way rather than go straight along
the main Carlisle-Glasgow road after our experience the previous
year when travelling in the opposite direction. Then, as we
approached Carlisle, I was concerned that our route involved
using the A74, an almost motorway-class dual carriageway, the
primary England-Scotland highway, a very fast and, for the
walker, a potentially very dangerous road.

No matter which way I held the map I could see no other
way round than to go through Longtown, a circuitous detour.
A further concern was that we were in Carlisle on a Friday,
always the busiest time of the week.

'One last try,' I said to Joan, 'we'll go to the police station
to see if there's any alternative'.

Complimenting myself on yet another brilliant idea we made
our way to the central police station. At the desk we attracted
the attention of the two duty constables and explained our
predicament.

'Wouldn't walk along the A74,' said the first constable.

'Not likely,' said his colleague, 'far too dangerous'.

'I'll ask the traffic sergeant,' said the first one, grabbing my
map. He returned fifteen minutes later.

'We cannot stop you,' said the first one, 'as it's not a
motorway it's not illegal, but we don't advise it'.

'Try the A7,' said the first one, looking at my map upside
down.

'Can't you walk over here,' said the second one, pointing

to the middle of the Solway Firth.

I was about to comment on my abilities to walk on water when from across the room a third voice chimed in, suggesting a ferry.

'Hang on a minute,' said the first one as he grabbed my map again and half of the Cumbria police force disappeared into a huddle.

More officers joined the crowd. Someone produced a wall map. Someone else produced a tray of steaming coffee cups as they settled down for a lengthy discussion on the various merits of my route planning. I glanced nervously at my watch, thinking that the gathering dusk would soon make the question of walking academic. Finally, from out of the assembled body, my map emerged like a rugby ball out of a scrum. The collective body straightened up from their hunched conversation and turned to face us. A decision had been made.

'Can't stop you using the A74,' said the first one with a deep baritone voice.

'Not against the law,' said the second one with a musical tenor voice.

'But we don't advise it,' chorused the others.

For some reason the symphony in my head was playing Gilbert and Sullivan's *The Pirates of Penzance*. We left the police station totally bemused. In a trance-like state we walked the three miles to the huge roundabout that is the junction with the M6, A74 and A7. With the chorus line, 'but we don't advise it, but we don't advise it' ringing around my head, I tossed a coin in the air and it came down heads, the M6. I tossed again, eliminating the M6 from my list of choices and it came down heads again. The A74. We walked into Scotland on that road and met Iain at the Gretna camp site in almost total darkness. When I planned the route for this year the coin came down tails. Hence we walked along the A7!

Now, back to the present and we approached Carlisle in ever increasing rain. The A7 is a very busy road but thankfully there was a footpath for most of the way so we were not playing Russian roulette with the traffic. Nine noisy and wet miles later and about half a mile from the busy, crowded centre of Carlisle a coach pulled up alongside us. It was one of the continental variety, heavily tinted windows, bright livery, toilet in the middle and about half a mile long.

Pulling up just in front of us a head appeared out of the

driver's window.

'Excuse Monsieur,' said the head, *'parlez vous francais?'* I groaned. I had just had a hard three weeks talking Scottish, French was completely beyond me. I shook my head in the same way Charles De Gaulle used to say 'Non' when Britain applied to join the Common Market.

A pair of shoulders appeared out of the window either side of the head. Two arms, one clutching a map, thrust their way out. The map was held in one hand whilst a Gauloise stained finger jabbed at it. I looked at the map, not sure whether it was a street map of Paris or Carlisle. Noting some of the roads had arrows on them indicating one way streets I deduced it was Carlisle.

My interest must have convinced the head that I had an encyclopaedic knowledge of the city for now retracted back into the coach, it turned and said something that made everyone cheer. I gave a Gallic shrug, trying to indicate I knew nothing. The shoulders returned the shrug enthusiastically. I raised my arms in just the way Francois Mitterrand did when talking to Margaret Thatcher. The arms attached to the shoulders enthusiastically raised themselves in reply, left higher than right. I raised my left higher in return and thrust my right out to say, 'Thanks and good luck'.

Arms, shoulders and head retracted back into the coach, the engine roared to life and the coach set off with the passengers all waving a cheerful greeting. For the first time I noticed there were two more identical coaches behind the first. In convoy they went off down the road, each one turning left behind the other.

We walked on. Passing the turning where the coaches had turned left, I noticed the last of the three was following the other two which had evidently turned first right. Why they should all be heading for the car park of a large supermarket was beyond me but with a Gallic shrug I strode on.

We reached the city centre and made for the pedestrian precinct, hoping to find a café. It was about lunchtime and everywhere was busy but eventually we found one with an empty table. As we took our dripping anoraks off, our brightly coloured sweatshirts with the girl in wheelchair and boy on crutches logo attracted a lot of interested stares. We sat down and I woke Joan up so she could choose from the menu. As it was her birthday I wanted to spoil her but she just fell asleep again. There was a crashing from the doorway and heads turned to the source of the noise. A severely spastic man pushing a wheelchair-bound lady was attempting to enter the café. Hands reached out to open the doors and with great difficulty they finally made an entry. The only table with spaces was ours so they came over. As the man stood there holding the wheelchair I looked at the logo on our shirts. It had just come to life.

People looked on with sympathy as the man clumsily sat down. I got the collection box out of the rucksack in anticipation of a generous response from the staring hordes and placed it on the table. The man looked at our shirts then at the collection box.

'What's it for?' said the man.

I explained the aims of the Star Centre.

'Can I go there?' said the man.

I explained it was for young people only. The man was obviously put out by this clinical rejection. His voice increased in volume. 'Don't believe in charity walks,' said the man.

Joan snapped awake. I explained it was a bit more than your usual 'three miles round the block' sponsored walk.

'Too many charity walks,' the man said louder, 'don't know what they are all for'.

Half the café stopped talking. I explained again that the Star Centre was a national, highly respected institution.

'Too many charities,' bellowed the man, 'not enough goes to those who need it,' as the other half of the café stopped talking.

Joan and I started to pack the rucksack. Hastily I cleared the collection box off the table.

'Too many people getting rake offs,' shouted the man as Joan spat her coffee all over the table. 'Don't know where all the money goes,' echoed the man as we hurried out of the café, Joan enjoying her birthday.

As we hastily left Carlisle I could not help but notice a convoy of brightly coloured coaches. The first had turned left off a roundabout and was turning first right whilst the other two were just leaving the roundabout. We walked up to where the A6 from Carlise meets the M6 and waited for Andy, who soon arrived on the scene. As we left for the camp site I saw three coaches turning left into an industrial estate.

We had only walked eighteen miles that day, Joan complaining of feeling tired, but it was her birthday and we were in England. Andy and Zoe had moved camp to the Eden Valley village of Englethwaite, about five miles from Carlisle. The Eden Valley is one of those undiscovered parts of England. Running roughly north to south from the Scottish Border to Penrith, it is virtually bypassed by the M6 and A6 running parallel to the east. The motorised traveller, hurtling along to fine things in Scotland or the Lake District, does not know what he is missing. Rolling hills fall into the exuberant Eden, cloaked in rich mixed woodland and concealing in their folds beautiful sleepy villages. The area contains every variety of scenery available, hills, rivers, forests, moorlands — all with the added benefit of very few tourists. It is a most enchanting place.

We reached the camp site and I woke Joan up so she could climb into the lorry and go to bed. Whilst Scotland has many attractions, the one thing that it desperately lacks is the equivalent of the English pub. After nearly three weeks of being starved of good beer and pleasant surroundings I looked forward to taking Joan out that night to such an institution. We were camping near the pleasant village of Armathwaite which boasts a selection of fine establishments, all serving good food from extensive menus. It was there we made our way in the evening. We were not disappointed. Beautiful surroundings, excellent food and fine beer were waiting to be sampled. Joan was feeling a bit too tired to really enjoy herself but with great enthusiasm I celebrated her birthday for her.

Throughout the walk Joan and I preferred where possible to wear training shoes. They have a number of advantages. Light in weight, comfortable, shock-absorbing soles and flexibility made them far superior to boots when walking on hard surfaces. Unfortunately trainers are not much use in very wet weather as they easily let in water and quickly become saturated. In wet conditions we had to resort to boots.

All our clothing was waterproofed with a substance called Goretex. It is a membrane bonded to outer and inner fabrics and has the enormous advantage of keeping water out whilst letting water vapour through. Until the recent development of Goretex and similar fabrics, all waterproof clothes suffered from condensation problems and an exercising body, producing litres of perspiration, would soon dampen the inside of clothing almost as much as adverse weather would dampen the outside. With Goretex this problem does not exist.

Waking up the next morning I could see our waterproofs were in for their first real test. So far we had averaged twenty-two miles a day, slightly ahead of schedule, and I wanted to keep it that way. Our ambitions for the day were to get past Penrith twenty miles away and perhaps reach the village of Askham five miles further on. Heavy rain drummed on the roof of the lorry. Sherry and Rocky, who both shared the lorry with us, indicated with their eyes that they were not too fussed about taking part in the day's exertions. We contemplated wearing our waterproof, lightweight tracksuits but another look outside convinced us it was heavy anorak and boots time.

Andy dropped us off at our finishing point the previous day and we soon had Carlisle behind us as we reached the A6. We had planned to take a scenic route, avoiding much of that busy and boring highway, but with the rain spoiling any view more than a hundred yards away we chose to stay on the A6 where there is at least a plentiful supply of pubs and cafés.

It rained all the way to Penrith. A handy café followed by a handy pub gave us an escape from the worst downpours but the persistent wet posed a stiff test for our waterproofs. For the first time since Dunnet Head we had to wear boots all day and it came as quite a shock to realise how tiring they were to wear when walking on hard paved or tarmacked surfaces. Equally we had to wear our waterproof coats all day and despite the unseasonally cold weather we quickly found it warm work.

We met with Zoe in Penrith and found yet another handy café to sit and plan our next moves in. We had achieved twenty miles that day and whilst it was less than we wanted I could see no point in getting wet for the sake of it. The need to wear boots and heavy anoraks made twenty miles seem like thirty. 'Thank goodness it's June,' I thought as I studied the map spread over a sticky table.

'This weather's not likely to stay like this for long,' I announced grandly, 'We'll call it a day now and leave the long days for when we get better weather.'

This decision was greeted with enthusiasm by Joan whose feet were struggling to come to terms with the unyielding boots that covered them. She gave me one of her 'My Hero who is Not Often Wrong' looks and helped me pack the rucksack. Zoe was equally cheerful, comparing the weather to that of her native North Queensland in the monsoon season. I began to realise why she looked so at home. So far we had been through cyclones at John o'Groats, searing heat in the Highlands and now monsoons. All we needed was the odd kangaroo hopping across the road to make her feel really at home.

We returned to the camp site, having avoided bumping into any stray marsupials. Andy, who had acted as chauffeur the previous night and had to remain sober, was looking forward to his first pint of decent beer in three weeks. Exercising the dogs that afternoon had been particularly arduous, both Sherry and Ben developing a liking for the wet, slimy, muddy conditions and rolling in every mud patch they came to.

'At least this weather is unlikely to last long, otherwise we would never finish,' said Andy, cleaning one unrecognisable canine with a mud-stained towel. I could only agree with him. Casting a seasoned eye towards the sky and explaining the presence of a slow moving occluded front, I knowledgably announced the probable presence of a high pressure front to the south-west, bringing fine weather with it. Joan gave me another My Hero look and didn't tell anyone that she had seen me reading that guff in a newspaper I had filched in one of our stopping points that morning. Fortunately I had chosen a career other than weather forecasting or I would be penniless by now.

'Treacle toffee day,' I said to Joan as we walked through Lowther Park, just outside Penrith. Following the downpour the day before, cold, grey, drizzly skies had replaced cold, grey abysmally wet ones. Lowther Park is part of the grounds of Lowther castle and provides three miles of pleasant, traffic-free walking. From there our route took us to the small village of Askham before disappearing down even quieter roads to the yet smaller village of Bampton. From there it was back to the A6 at Shap village, then to the pass of the same name.

The previous year in similar conditions, thirsty and hungry, we had called at the local post office in Askham and bought sweets and drinks. This was a lucky find. The treacle toffee I bought then was the finest I had ever tasted. Now as we approached Askham I looked forward to renewing that delectable relationship. We went to the post office and sure enough, on a shelf behind the counter, was the dark brown nectar.

'I'll have those,' I said to the woman, indicating all six packets on the shelf. Startled, she recovered and handed them over.

'Got any more?' I enquired.

She disappeared to the stockroom and came back with a half empty box.

'I'll have those,' I said to the woman, indicating the remaining bags. She blinked and then handed over six more packets.

'Got any more?' I enquired, stuffing the packets in the rucksack.

'She hesitated, convinced herself that there had been no reports of escaped madmen that morning, went into the stockroom and reappeared, carrying another box. I started to pack the rucksack. Seeing my lips start to move she pre-empted the question with a shake of the head.

'No more,' she said numbly, holding the counter tight.

With bulging rucksack and teeth glued together with treacle toffee we made our way out of Askham, Joan lightening my load by giving my lunchtime apple to a horse that in turn rejected my offer of a treacle toffee. Nine miles after leaving Penrith we came to the village of Bampton, on the edge of the Lake District, and then skirting Haweswater, the most easterly of the lakes, we made our way to the village of Shap. A quick phone call to Zoe, telling her where to meet us, and we dived into a café for tea and welcome shelter from the rain.

Zoe, coming from Down Under sometimes had a problem with her innate direction finding. An hour later we were still in the café with no sign of Zoe. She and Andy had moved camp that morning from Carlisle to Kendal, to the south, and I was concerned that something had gone wrong.

Joan returned to the phone box and came back a few minutes later with the sort of look on her face that could melt steel. She sat down and a few minutes later said, 'She's in Lancaster,' having calmed down sufficiently to talk. Zoe, instead of being twenty miles north of Kendal, was in fact twenty miles south. Her Antipodean feet and Antipodean head had become confused. She had headed south on the M6, started to question where she was, gone into Lancaster and started to look for Shap. An hour later, just as Joan and I were enjoying our twenty-third cup of tea, she appeared.

It had stopped raining and Zoe had thoughtfully put our trainers in the Land Rover. We changed footwear and I was also grateful for the chance to jettison a heavy, bulging rucksack. Two hours and seven miles later and we were on top of Shap pass, the dreaded steep climb that before being bypassed by the

M6 was responsible for miles of traffic jams as heavy lorries struggled to its summit on the way to or from Scotland.

The usual gale was blowing when we reached the summit. Shap is actually part of a long ridge running laterally off the Pennines and connecting with the easterly Lake District fells. It is the highest point for miles around, too high for trees to grow, and consequently there is nothing to break the wind.

A sparse landscape also does things to my bladder. The numerous cups of tea I had drunk in Shap were now coming to the end of the plumbing system. In that barren place, with no shelter for miles around, with hordes of curious people driving up and down the road, something had to happen. The only 'decency shelter' for miles was the Land Rover so, after parking it at a crazy angle to the road, poor Zoe had to get out and go for a walk whilst I made use of its kerbside screen.

Able at last to think comfortably, I looked at the map, whilst Zoe, now free to splash around, poured yet more tea from a steaming vacuum flask. So far we had managed nineteen miles. We were going well and six miles down the road was a pub with a large car park, an ideal location at an ideal distance. Despatching Zoe to find the pub and with the wind bringing the threat of more rain, we set off. A few miles of downhill walking and with ominous clouds building up in the sky we reached the pub and Zoe. Another look at the map and we decided to return to Kendal, satisfied with a twenty-five mile day despite adverse conditions.

I woke up several times during the night, disturbed by the sound of rain beating against the lorry roof. We sleepily staggered from the camp site the next day and were dropped off at the pub car park, the heavy rain causing big puddles to form. Feet once more clad in unyielding boots, we set off downhill towards Kendal. The rain got heavier, Goretex struggling to keep the deluge at bay. We reached Kendal and found a café.

'Can't get worse,' I said to Joan, as we drank our fourth cup tea whilst our coats, suspended on hooks, were creating a mini lake by dripping into the well for the door mat. Yet again my talents for weather forecasting were to prove to be abysmally pathetic. As we left Kendal the heavens opened as if someone up there had said, 'You ain't seen nothing yet.' We hadn't.

Three miles out of Kendal we stopped at the camp site which

was on route. After two hours of sheltering from the torrents we decided to brave the elements again. Stepping out of the lorry we almost disappeared into ground rapidly taking on the consistency of a mangrove swamp. We splashed our way out of the camp site and four miles later splashed our way into the small town of Milnthorpe. The rain was so heavy it was difficult to see ten yards ahead.

At Milnthorpe we called it a day. It was not the damp that stopped us for we were not wet, Goretex had reigned supreme. Nor was it having to walk along, hoods pulled over eyes, obscuring vision, eyes straining downwards at boots to shelter from stinging rain, swamped with tidal waves each time a car or lorry passed. It was the sheer boredom. The sheer depressing inability to see anything, appreciate anything, hear anything, say anything. For the first time the weather had beaten us. Having survived storm force winds, burning sun, heat exhaustion, blisters and overdoses of tea and treacle toffee, we finished a day without reaching our chosen objective.

'Can't last long,' I said to Joan, without any real conviction and secure in the knowledge that it could.

That night, as we made plans for the following morning, Joan and I agreed that we must walk at least twenty-one miles, regardless of weather. A few more days at fourteen miles a day would soon put us behind schedule.

'Tomorrow, come hell or high water, we must be south of Lancaster,' I said firmly.

Joan gave me a 'You are So Masterful' look and contemplated the 'high water' bit.

Our return to Milnthorpe was made in grim silence; even Andy driving the Land Rover seemed to have caught our mood. Arriving at our start point, we cast a weather eye around. It was bright sunshine but a cold, blustery wind told us it was not going to stay dry for long. We tossed a coin; it came down tails so we put our boots on and set off down the A6, Joan with her jaw set tight with determination, me with a jaw glued tight with treacle toffee. Two miles from our start point in Milnthorpe we turned off the A6 for beautifully quiet roads bordering Morecambe Bay. Despite the sunshine there was still a lot of water around and as we went along wooded lanes the wind shook the trees and the wet foliage poured water on our heads.

Eight miles from Milnthorpe we reached Carnforth, famous

to many as an important railway junction in the pioneering days of steam but to Joan it was famous as the home of a second hand bookshop that reputedly stocks 10,000 books. Joan is an avid book reader and it was only the threat of more impending rain that kept her from trying to read a reputed 10,000 titles.

I was grateful to Joan for opting to spend a little bit of time book hunting. For many days now I had accepted cramped and weak legs, sore and numb feet, as a lesser evil than the agonising pain that appeared each time I relented on taking drugs. Wearing boots had exacerbated the problem and I had eventually reached a point where legs were ceasing to work. A few minutes of painful massage produced some life but it was obvious that I was going to have to take a rest from the pills and potions if I was going to be able to continue.

From Carnforth, in increasing rain, we again abandoned our ambitions of following a pretty route and chose to trudge to Lancaster along the A6. It is an unattractive road, passing through ribbon developments almost all of the way between the two towns and giving the appearance of a continuous walk through urban areas. Whilst being bypassed by the M6, the road still attracts a substantial amount of traffic and it was a dirty, smelly and noisy walk to Lancaster.

Joan and I liked living in the Lancaster area. Close to the Yorkshire Dales in the east and the Lake District in the north it makes an ideal tourist centre, whilst on the immediate doorstep are the sands of Morecambe Bay and the gentle beauty of the Lune Valley. It has a pleasant city centre, and historic old castle, a brewery and a good selection of cosmopolitan restaurants. As we approached the familiar surroundings it started to rain. As the light rain began to become heavy rain we found a café and sat down to a pot of tea just as the heavens opened. Thinking of our good fortune in narrowly avoiding another drenching I thought back to the previous year when we had passed through the area.

We had reached Caton, in the Lune Valley near Lancaster. Local knowledge of the area had assisted us in planning a route through some outstandingly beautiful countryside. The weather was warm. The camp site had a small hotel attached and we went there for a drink. The bar was deserted except for one other person. I looked, Joan looked, but neither of us said anything, respecting a TV star's desire for anonymity. Iain walked in.

With the subtlety of a sledgehammer he said 'Hey! Aren't you Jim Bowen?' to the well known comedian and host of ITV's popular game show, *Bullseye*! Jim Bowen is a marvellous, genuine person and for the next four hours he gave us the pleasure of his most humorous company. As we sat watching rivulets of water run down the café windows I wished Jim Bowen could be with us now, cheering us up.

The rain didn't last long. With a faint glimpse of the sun we grabbed our coats and dashed out of the café only to collide with two people holding a gallon bucket of wet money.

'Collecting for charity,' gushed the first.

'Land's End to John o'Groats,' gushed the second.

'On bikes,' panted the first. 'Relay ride, eighteen people,' enthusiastically gushed the two young faces with water dripping off cold, red noses.

I resisted the temptation to mug the competition, I didn't need a gallon bucket that badly.

'Where are you from?' Joan asked.

'Bristol,' gushed the first.

'Students,' gushed the second.

'What's the worthy cause?' I asked.

'Two main causes,' they said in a synchronised gush. 'The first one is research into Alzheimer's disease.'

I looked at Joan, perhaps in need of it. Joan caught my look, unamused.

'The second one is the homeless in Bristol.'

Joan returned my look; I was definitely in need of that one. We told them that there were only two of us, not eighteen, we were walking, not riding and if they got blisters like Joan gets blisters then don't expect to sit down for a long time.

As we walked out of Lancaster I thought of Joan's blisters and the corresponding equation that blisters on the bum divided by eighteen is probably not too painful. As we left Lancaster the rain eased, then stopped altogether. The sun came out, a rare commodity. We were met by Andy a few miles out and changed into our beloved trainers. Ditching the rucksack and waterproof coats, we turned off the A6 onto a small road that took us past Lancaster University and into the village of Galgate and back on the A6. From Galgate we were able to leave the A6 in favour of a network of small roads that took us to Cabus, a small village just outside Garstang. There we stopped for the day. We had walked twenty-seven miles in variable weather but fortunately had escaped the worst bit, courtesy of a rather nice café. In twenty-four days we had walked 529 miles. By my calculations we were now exactly half way.

We were getting quite adept at interpreting the television weather person's phraseology. A 'pulse' of rain meant you could get wet any time but it wouldn't last long. 'Showers' meant you could get wet from three or more connected pulses. 'Showers, some prolonged and heavy,' meant swim for it. 'A band' of rain was drizzle all day. 'A heavy band' was a lot of prolonged, heavy showers whilst the 'chance of even heavier bursts of rain' meant find the high ground and stay there. Andy, moving camp from Kendal to Garstang, had just dropped us off at Cabus on a day that promised 'a heavy band of rain crossing the region'. We set off in trainers, not expecting rain till later.

Breakfast was often a problem to Joan and I. Not always feeling like something first thing, and often anxious to get out to make the most of patches of dry weather, we would often end up walking miles on empty stomachs.

'First café we come to, we'll stop and get breakfast,' I said masterfully to Joan through a mouthful of treacle toffee, as we waved goodbye to Andy. Joan nodded in agreement and gave me a 'You're so Masterful' look before taking her first tentative steps on painful feet.

We set off down twenty yards of quiet lane to the A6. Turning left I collided with a big sign that said CAFE. I turned to negotiate change of terms with Joan, perhaps the next café after the next. I was too late. Joan was already giving her order in.

'Come far today,' enquired the waitress.

'About twenty bbnnmmmm' I mumbled, hurriedly stuffing a piece of toast in my mouth.

'How far?' queried the waitress.

'About twenty mmmnnn,' I mumbled again, ramming another piece of toast in my mouth.

The waitress gave Joan a look of admiration that was her cue to take the collection box out of the rucksack. I heard the waitress talking to another customer.

'About twenty,' she said, 'and it's still only nine o'clock.'

'How far?' queried another customer.

'Not yet half past nine,' said another voice.

Murmurings of 'about twenty,' 'ten before six o'clock,' 'forty by lunchtime,' began to ripple through the café. I kept my head low in case someone had seen us getting out of the Land Rover five minutes ago. As customers left large donations began to crash into the collection box, admiring glances shone our way.

Twenty minutes later we were leaving the café with full stomachs and an even fuller collection box. A few miles later, as we started to walk through Garstang, it began to rain.

'My feet are getting wet,' I said to Joan who was walking underneath a 'pulse' of rain.

'Only a heavy shower,' said Joan as a 'burst' bounced off my head.

A little while later and it was dawning on both of us that 'the heavy band' had arrived. Drenched, we came to a pub and, crossing through another pulsating band of heavy, prolonged showers, we burst into it. Joan ordered drinks whilst I found a telephone and got through to Zoe with a message to bring a change of clothing. Even though we were wet through I felt we were fortunate for we just got into shelter when the rain intensified as even heavier bursts crossed the region. Zoe came and whilst she ordered more drinks and food Joan and I changed into boots and heavy waterproofs.

Two hours later the rain eased sufficiently for us to start walking again. As we reached Preston the rain stopped and we were able to navigate our way through the centre of town on some minor roads, an impossible feat in heavy rain as it was necessary to constantly refer to the map, which would have quickly dissolved if exposed to such wet conditions.

In the centre of Preston is Moor Park, where we had arranged to meet Zoe. It was an oasis of peace and quiet that was desperately needed as we rejoined the traffic thundering along the major vehicular arteries that pass through the town. As we approached the centre of Preston the searing pain that had started twenty minues earlier got out of control. I reached Moor Park and collapsed in a screaming heap. For the next hour startled passers by were treated to the sight of a jabbering idiot clad in a bright yellow jersey screaming and banging his head on the ground.

Zoe arrived in the middle of this performance but I found it impossible to get into the car. The pain was so intense the only relief I could get was to stamp up and down or kneel on hands and knees, banging my head on the floor. Not for the first time we were confronted by strangers offering to ring for an ambulance or rush to get a doctor. Each time Joan had to patiently explain to these concerned and kind people that the attack would be over in an hour or two hours and the best that anyone could do was to ensure I had room to breathe, freedom to move around and plenty of water to drink. On this occasion the water was not a problem; deluges of the stuff were falling out of the sky again.

Eventually the pain subsided and so did the rain. There was no point continuing. I was so weak I could barely stand and the nagging pain left after the attack had ceased would continue for many hours. We had managed over twenty-one miles so we were able to return to the camp site reasonably satisfied with the day.

Sherry is a slob. Leave a dustbin uncovered, she's in it. Find a pile of dung somewhere, she's in it. Find a pool of water somewhere, she's in it. Not clean wholesome soapy water. Mention 'bath' and her eyes roll back into her head, thoughts of leaving home flit across her brain, ideas of ringing Amnesty International and laying a complaint of torture come into her head. It's got to be dirty, foul, evil smelling water, the more stagnant the better.

The camp site we were staying at was adjacent to a marina serving the boating fraternity who like to potter up and down the Lancaster Canal. Andy found the banks of the marina and the canal an ideal place to exercise the dogs. Ben could run up and down sniffing the mooring ropes for other dogs, Rocky could investigate all the tiny holes made by water rats and other creatures and ... Sherry just couldn't resist it. The water smelled right, stagnant, it looked right, muddy, and it was easy to get into; just slyly walk off the bank whilst Andy's not looking. Even better, there was a handy shelf that allowed her to wallow in two foot of water. Not deep enough to sink in but deep enough to wallow in.

Andy turned round and all of a sudden, no Sherry. A call to Rocky and Ben soon produced two happy and relatively sweet smelling dogs, but no sign of Sherry. He started to search the canal bank until the sound of splashing water alerted him to the spot where the missing canine could be found, covered from head to foot in the foulest water anywhere in the canal. Wondering how he was possibly going to get that evil smelling thing clean and presentable, his problem was compounded by Rocky.

Terriers normally are not too keen on getting wet, their coat being too thin and short to keep them warm when wet. However, Rocky loves Sherry. Anything Sherry can do, Rocky can do. With a spring and a bounce he launched himself off the towpath to be with his best friend.

Comedy now nearly became tragedy. Rocky missed the ledge and ended up in the full depth of the canal. In a panic he thrashed around and disappeared under an adjacent boat. Andy was now lying face down, nose six inches from the foul smelling water, trying desperately to get hold of Rocky's collar. Rocky was trapped under water, sandwiched between boat and bank. Andy, both arms in the water, in the nick of time found Rocky's ears, then his neck, then his collar and with a desperate heave pulled a frightened and bewildered mutt from under the boat to safety.

By the time we rejoined Andy he had managed to clean two evil smelling dogs. Unfortunately he had not had time to clean himself. Not wishing to say anything, we gave Andy strange looks, wrinkling our noses at the wafts of evil smells emanating from him. When he suggested we all eat in the caravan, we suggested back to Andy that he eat in the caravan, we'll eat out. Over dinner Andy told us the story. Sighing with relief at understanding the source of the smell, we gently suggested to Andy that a change of clothes would not go amiss!

Joan's feet were now beginning to heal although she was still troubled by new blisters. The constant wet weather was giving me some concern that things could once again deteriorate. Wear trainers and the feet get wet, recipe for more blisters. Alternatively, wear boots and the more unyielding sole also aggravates blistered feet. When planning the following day's exertions we had to constantly balance the desire to walk much longer distances with the need to protect the feet from adverse conditions as much as possible. Now there were other things to contend with. Recurring bouts of neuralgia during the night had left me walking on legs cramped with drugs and a body exhausted from frequent bouts of pain and only two hours' sleep.

Even though we were both capable of walking well in excess of twenty miles a day, it was that distance I decided on for the following day. Whilst being sufficient to get us clear of the Preston and central Lancashire urban area, it was short enough to give Joan's feet another chance to heal despite the damp conditions and probably the maximum I could manage on legs knotted with excruciating cramp. I was still sure that fine weather could arrive any time and that would be the cue for extending distances.

Preston was another area that we knew well. In over twenty years of marriage that has seen many career and house moves, we have an almost encyclopaedic knowledge of many parts of the country. The main road south from Preston is the A6 which, on its way to Manchester, crosses through the heavily industrialised areas of Leyland, Chorley, Adlington and the industrial west Manchester edge. To the west of the A6 is the central Lancashire coal mining belt and to the east is the Pennines. We went east. The weatherman had promised sunny intervals with a few showers and it was in a sunny interval that we left Preston. Three miles of urban streets and we were in a café at Bamber Bridge, south of Preston, eating bacon sandwiches whilst a shower made a mess of our sunny interval. It didn't last long and under grey skies we left the sanctuary of the café and continued down the A6.

Shortly after leaving the café we were able to leave main roads behind by following a network of unclassified roads that shortly left the urban sprawl and climbed steeply to an area of open moorland. Fairly soon we were rewarded with extensive views across the valley that contains reservoirs in a beautiful park-like setting. The tiny road that skirts this moorland then drops steeply to the Anglezarke and Rivington reservoirs.

At a car park specially created to take advantage of the outstanding views, we met up again with Andy. We were trying to keep in training shoes and light waterproofs and, now that we had left the urban areas and with it cafés, pubs, churches and bus shelters, wanted the security of knowing that in a sudden deluge help was not far behind. We refreshed ourselves with tea and sandwiches and then set off for the remaining six miles to Horwich. Andy also set off for Horwich as an advance party to seek out a café.

It was now drizzling but insufficiently to dampen shoes or hearts. We had skirted a huge cleft in the hillside called Anglezarke Quarry, a disused working which, many years previously, I used to fall off with amazing regularity, as it is now a rock climber's playground. We then came to Leverhulme

Park. Donated by the Leverhulme family, it is many square miles of mixed woods and meadow, a favourite riding area and a green lung to the west of the heavily industrialised North Lancashire cotton belt.

At the end of the park a little while later we were in Horwich. This small town is at the north-west extremity of the arc of towns that forms the Lancashire cotton belt and which, in the vibrant days of the Empire at the turn of the century, contributed so much to the nation's wealth. Pressed hard against the steep slopes of the Pennines, the towns of Bolton, Bury, Heywood, Rochdale, Oldham, Shaw, Ashton and other smaller villages run in arc north to south-east of Manchester. Each town, whilst principally involved in spinning, also specialised in different areas and in Horwich there were mills whose principal activities were bleaching and dyeing. Whilst the nation became wealthy, for those whose livelihood depended upon the mill, times were hard. Long working hours, lungs clogged by fine cotton dust, poor, cramped housing and an unhealthy climate contributed to a vast catalogue of diseases that ensured a short, uncomfortable life for most. In 1832, when the first factory act relating to the textile mills was passed, it was estimated that fifty seven per cent of children in the Manchester area died before the age of five. Communities became dependent on each other, the Co-operative movement was formed in Rochdale, and the warmth and honesty for which the Lancastrian is noted was born in these harsh conditions.

Now King Cotton is largely dead. The demise of the Empire left many Third World nations with the technology to spin their own cotton and new man-made fibres have reduced the demand for the natural fibre. The cotton towns have shrunk into poverty and deprivation. New industries may have taken over, new technology may have breathed some life back into the moribund cotton industry, but there is still high unemployment. As we were to find out, there is also still that pride, that warmth and that humanity.

As we walked into Horwich we were reminded why cotton was brought to the region in the first place. The weather. Cotton fibres are very friable and friability increases as the fibre dries. To successfully spin it the fibre needs to be kept moist and the high average humidity in the East Lancashire Pennine area provides an ideal climate. The stories of rainy Manchester were born of fact, not myth.

It started to rain as we met Andy and he guided us to a small café in the market area of Horwich. Not for the first time we were fortunate in reaching shelter just before the heavens opened. As we drunk our way through interminable cups of tea an elderly man asked were we walking from John o'Groats to Land's End. We replied and explained about the Star Centre. Without hesitation he emptied every penny of change he had into our collection box. Other people noted and did likewise. The proprietor put £5 in, as did someone else. It was a humbling experience to watch these kind, honest people help those making a real effort to help those worse off. It eventually stopped raining and we said our goodbyes to our new found friends in that café. A few more miles and our day's objective was reached despite adverse weather. We returned to the camp site satisfied with the day and with a bulging collection box.

By arriving in Horwich we had at last deviated from the route taken the previous year. With a few exceptions we had so far followed in reverse our previous year's route. Then from Angelzarke we passed through the West Lancashire mining areas of Wigan, Golborne and Warrington and then through West Cheshire and Shropshire. This year we were following a route further to the east. This, I hoped, would introduce more variety and quieter roads than the miles of urban streets we had tramped along previously.

One memorable incident relieved the monotony of our urban route. Cold, wet weather, the most uninspiring countryside we had yet walked through and painful feet had dampened our spirits. The urban streets had dried our throats and we were in need of refreshment. We had been tramping dusty streets for miles without finding a café and were beginning to hallucinate about vast, steaming pots of tea.

We were now in the outskirts of Wigan. Turning a corner we came across a corner shop that looked like a prop from Coronation Street. In disbelief we looked at the sign — 'Grocers, tobacconist, off sales, teas and coffees'. I blinked and looked again. Teas, coffees — I really was hallucinating. Joan convinced me I wasn't. We crossed the road and went in.

'Are you serving teas?' I asked.

The proprietor reeled back in shock at being asked such a stupid question. It was April, winter had barely gone, the glaciers had barely retreated, what sort of strange people could want tea this early in the season? He surveyed the weary pair in front of him. Convinced it was a genuine enquiry he then recovered his composure. Taking a deep breath he indicated with his eyes a pile of rusting garden furniture, then the wet and windy street outside. We equally indicated with our eyes that a pavement café in freezing downtown Wigan was not our idea of fun. Unperturbed and determined not to let a customer down he then proceeded to erect the rusting table and chairs amongst the rows of tinned peas. For the next half hour we demurely sipped tea alongside the bacon counter whilst astonished customers came and went. The next ten miles of painful walking on urban streets were greatly relieved by the memory of this most eccentric incident.

Now, as then, the weather was wet. Only our route had changed. Andy dropped us off in Horwich on his way to the next camp site near a small village called Rixton, to the east of Warrington. We left Horwich and through wet streets tramped along in boot clad feet. For the second day I was having to contend with a sleepless night and it was in robotic fashion that I tramped the urban pavements.

As with all urban areas local road planning was playing havoc with my navigation. What the map indicated as a perfectly logical road junction was made a mess of by a local one way system that appeared designed to funnel traffic away from the area as efficiently as possible. I couldn't help thinking the traffic needed little encouragement to make its escape from row after row of drab urban streets.

I was even less impressed on reaching a place called Hulton Park only to find that the secluded grounds of a large manor house were anything but the public park I had been anticipating. the map showed a handy track running diagonally across the park but large signs carrying the usual warning about trespassers ending up as shark bait encouraged me to walk around the outside instead.

A few miles and we reached a handy pub in a downpour. the pub sign showed a rugby league player in a distinctive hooped Jersey. My map told me we were in a district called Leigh, which boasts a famous Rugby League side, so whilst Joan went in search of a much needed 'Ladies', I made pleasant conversation with some people at the bar, talking about the local side in reverential terms.

My knowledge of Rugby League is not that great. As one after another of the locals joined in dispute about who the greatest team in the world was, I began to wish that I had kept my big mouth shut. Slowly my brain perceived the notion that the hooped jersey worn by the player on the sign belongs to Wigan, arch rivals of Leigh. Joan returned and this gave me an opportunity to change the subject to stamp collecting.

The downpour ceased and we made our way once more. Another few miles and we were approaching an area of low lying peat moor known as Chat Moss. Nothing ever really happened to Chat Moss until the dawn of the industrial revolution. Then the two great centres of British commerce, Liverpool and Manchester, decided it would be a good idea if they were connected by a railway. George Stevenson was appointed surveyor and then engineer for this pioneering line and fairly quickly he found the natural line blocked by the oozing, soggy black sponge of 'the moss'. His answer was to raise an embankment built upon a raft of faggots to spread the weight of the proposed four and a half ton locomotives. This solution was treated with scorn by many of his contemporaries but the gallant Geordie went ahead. Today trains of 400 tons thunder over his embankment. The fist train, the *Northumbrian*, crossed Chat Moss in 1830 and opened the world's first ever passenger railway line.

Today, apart from the railway, only farm tracks cross the moss, their being no through road north to south. I looked forward to a few miles of peace and quiet but soon the rain, first a drizzle, started to spoil my day. We reached a level crossing and Joan wanted to wait for a train to come along. She had read somewhere that the rails bounce up and down with the weight of the locomotive pressing on the spongy surface. I was really amused by this. It was quite warm and we had decided to leave heavy waterproofs behind in favour of our lightweight, Goretex-proofed tracksuits. Whilst affording reasonable protection in average rain these waterproofs struggled in the sort of downpours known as 'heavy pulses'. Now, as I looked at the black, weeping sky I wondered how long I would wait for a bouncing train to come along. As I chewed on treacle toffee my prayers were answered. We craned our necks to see the pogo stick on rails. The train flashed by, remarkably level, no sway, no bounce and what looked to be no passengers. We turned away and in increasingly heavy rain made our way to the twin towns of Irlam and Cadishead.

I had planned to avoid most of the ugly sprawl of the two towns by following a track marked clearly on the map. Now standing looking in the direction of our planned route, I changed my mind. There must have been at least twenty signs, stretching into the distance, gently encouraging people to find an alternative way. 'No Entry', 'Private', Beware of Dogs', 'We Prosecute Trespassers', 'Only One Warning Shot will be Fired', 'Beware of Mines', 'Trespassers will be turned into Fertiliser', the warnings were endless. With a shrug of damp shoulders we turned and headed for the attractions of Irlam.

Not even the most fanatical devotee of Irlam would agree it is attractive. In fact it is drab beyond belief. A ribbon of houses, industrial estates, chemical works and pubs, it is sandwiched between the Manchester Ship Canal and Chat Moss. Subjected to the usual graffiti-led vandalism, it has the air of a rundown cemetery. The rain now moved into the category of torrential, what the weatherpeople call 'showers, sometimes prolonged and heavy'. As we walked under the railway bridge where bold letters told the world that 'John loves Mary' and 'Reds Rule OK' my thoughts were on ringing Andy or Zoe and saying, 'Come and get us.' Joan resisted. 'You can only get wet once,' she said. 'Can't get any wetter,' she said a bit later. 'If it was easy everyone would do it,' a bit later still. With that encouragement from a partner whose feet must have been agonisingly painful, who was I to argue.

We splashed on and duly reached Rixton, the camp site and Zoe and Andy struggling with a pile of steaming washing. We gratefully added to their misery by peeling off our wet clothes and adding them to the 'To be Washed' pile. We had completed just over eighteen miles that day, a disappointing total but at least we were now south of the Greater Manchester industrialised area. An early finish to the day was also a welcome relief to a body starved of sleep and exhausted by constant pain. Swallowing another handful of pills I collapsed onto the bed to get a brief respite before starting the evening exertions of meeting with Joan's family who lived just the other side of Manchester.

Middle England

Day twenty-eight dawned bright and cheerful as a sunny interval paid us a visit. So far we had walked 591 miles, an average before today of just under twenty-two miles a day. We were slightly ahead of target but really needed a few good days of walking to get our noses comfortably in front. The sunshine streaming through the steamy windows fuelled my optimism. Joan's feet were healing well and surely this sunshine must herald a change to some more seasonally average June weather.

We left the camp site with feet clad in trainers and bodies clad in light waterproofs, a declaration of our new found optimism. The previous night we were joined by some of Joan's family who are natives of the region. We celebrated well and my head was now exacting retribution. As I hoped that lungfuls of fresh air would clear away the reminders of the night before, we left Rixton by a small toll road that crosses the Manchester Ship Canal, passed through the village of Warburton and, still enjoying a sunny interval, we looked forward to some very quiet roads taking us to the Cheshire town of Knutsford.

Enjoying the break from rain we rounded a bend and found what the rain had left behind. A puddle. Not your average puddle but a lake stretching the width of the road for about a hundred yards and of variable depth. We were both wearing trainers. I consulted the oracle, a very soggy example of an Ordnance Survey Landranger series map. Retreat would involve two miles of retraced steps followed by a three mile detour. The inland sea had to be crossed. If there was a time to perfect the art of walking on water, this was it.

'Let me lead the way,' I said heroically to Joan, who gave me a 'My Hero, You're Welcome' look. I gingerly moved to the edge of the inland sea. A long stride and I was precariously balanced on a rock. Joan waited for the splash. It didn't come. Recovering my balance I now managed to step to the edge, falling into some sharp brambles. I helped Joan follow in my footsteps. We stood there and looked at our new position. From the edge of the inland sea I had managed to get us into the middle of it! Her face said it all. 'Brilliant! Stuck in the middle of a puddle. Which way now mastermind?'

I looked at the water in front of me, concentrating, trying to see a way through. I stepped forward onto a half submerged rock, then another rock, a wobble as I put my weight on it, concentration now intense, head down, leaping for another unsteady dry spot; sweat running in my eyes, I tiptoed round the edge. Sucking sound as my right foot found a soft spot, gurgles as I pulled it out, stained and dripping. Another death defying leap, rocking, swaying, steadying for another leap, squelch from soggy feet, splash as I fell short. End now in sight, teeth clenched, eyes down in concentration, one more leap, a small step for mankind and I was there! Wet, stained, strained but triumphant! I turned to call Joan over but found she had arrived, dry, smiling and smug, having found a dry ridge the other side of the boundary hedge and calmly walked over.

With squelching foot we neared Knutsford. At the small village of Egerton there is a youth club and it was having an open day. Noticing the bit that said Teas, Coffees, Cakes we went in.

The lady serving teas, noting the logo on our shirts, enquired about our walk. Handing over the teas she refused payment, insisting we have those on the house. Another lady brought over some cake, insisting we must be hungry and have this one on the house. A man brought over some more cake whilst a lady wrapped up even more goodies in a bag so that we could take some with us. We drank more tea, then eventually got up to leave. As if all the generosity had not been good enough we were pursued by a man who insisted we take a £5 donation with us. At this point the sun shone both on us and in us. We reached Knutsford and made arrangements to meet Andy. A pulse of rain appeared and we burst into a café. Whilst drinking tea the proprietor came over and asked about our walk. 'Have those on me,' he said, also passing the menu over.

We met Andy who had changed into Zoe. Andy had originally taken the call whilst doing some washing in a launderette.

Unable to leave his washed once, spun twice and now tumbling dry laundry, Zoe had to take over. Keeping to a point never far from us, she went ahead, stocking up with water and other refreshments. We walked on. Cheshire is mostly flat country and large man-made objects tend to dominate the skyline. This was now the case with the huge dome of Jodrell Bank Radio Telescope. Mile after mile and in ever threatening rain the dome grew nearer. As a few spots of rain started to fall we eventually reached the futuristic dishes.

Looking at that eerie dome, 250 feet in diameter and over 300 feet high, I was reminded of the determination of the originator, Sir Bernard Lovell. 'He wouldn't be put off by a drop of rain,' I thought. It was in 1945 that Dr A.C.B. Lovell obtained temporary permission from Manchester University to use some of their horticultural land at Jodrell Bank. The theory that far off stars could be 'seen' in electro-magnetic forms other than visible light was well known but had never been practically proved and at that time the technology to achieve it was but a pipe dream of astronomers. Dr Lovell, soon to become Professor Lovell, had scrounged some bits or war surplus, namely advanced field radar sets, and having set them up in the midst of the Botany Department's fields, he set out to demonstrate that cosmic rays could be detected by the radio frequencies they emitted. He failed to find cosmic rays but detected instead a series of cosmic showers. This was the birth of radio astronomy.

Jodrell Bank is owned by Manchester University and is not state funded. In 1947 after more successful demonstrations, Professor Lovell and Manchester University started to build the world's first astrological radio telescope. By 1957, after many setbacks and many frustrations, it began to seem a doomed white elephant. Despite being close to completion there was a shortfall of funds and sponsorship was desperately required. At the time there were many rumours that the Russians were experimenting with spacecraft but this was in the most icy period of the cold war and information on what was happening east of the Iron Curtain was hard to come by. By tuning the incomplete detectors to the right frequency and pointing the incomplete dish in the right direction, Jodrell Bank astounded the world by detecting the carrier rocket for the Sputnik One spacecraft before the Russians could announce their own triumph. With the world's attention now focussed on them, Professor Lovell and his team obtained the necessary sponsorship from the Nuffield Foundation.

In 1961 the world's first ever radio telescope became fully operational under the command of the one man whose genius, determination and tenacity saw the project through from conception to completion. It is ironic that recently the staff at Manchester University have confirmed Jodrell Bank as a world leader by making the first ever discovery of a planet outside our own solar system. This is a gigantic leap forward in the 'life on other planets' debate and the discovery has been hailed worldwide as a staggering achievement. In the same month it was announced by Manchester University that they may have to close down the telescope due to shortage of funds!

As we left the eerie dish behind I thought of Sir Bernard and those early cosmic showers. 'How did he know they were showers?' I wondered. 'They may have been cosmic pulses, perhaps a band of meteorites crossing the galaxy. Did they have sunny, perhaps infra-red, intervals? How did he know it was not a prolonged period of cosmic disturbance with the chance of heavy showers, some of them thundery. Was that lightning or a pulsar?'

I was disturbed in my cosmic thoughts by a very terrestrial drop of rain falling on my very mortal head. We were walking on some blissfully quiet roads and soon reached the village of Brownlow Heath in South Cheshire. We had said goodbye to Lancashire, were nearly out of Cheshire and into the Potteries. We had walked twenty-eight miles and ended this most satisfying day on a high note.

The following day Andy dropped us off before continuing with the caravan to our next camp site, at Trentham Park near Newcastle-under-Lyme. The heavy rain that had arrived as we finished the previous evening had continued throughout the night and was now digging in to continue through the day. This was no 'lightweight' day and clad once more in boots and anorak we set off for another wet and tiring walk.

A couple of miles trudging brought us to the A34 at Scholar Green, a few miles from Newcastle-under-Lyme. The road was wet, the footpath narrow, the traffic heavy. As the first heavy lorry sped past a bow wave of dirty black water swamped us. Twenty bow waves later we decided to have a sheltered break somewhere.

'Pub over there,' Joan shouted, above the roar of the traffic. We crossed the road to the pub, The Travellers Rest. It was closed. No rest for travellers. We trudged on. A sodden fag packet, carried aloft on a muddy brown tidal wave, slid down my leg. We reached the district called Red Bull. I don't know what came first, the district or the pub, but the place of refreshment that we stepped into wasn't called the Brown Cow!

It was in 1759 that Josiah Wedgewood founded a small pottery business which developed into the internationally renowned company that today still bears his name. The success of Wedgewood was matched by others and soon the five towns of Stoke, Burslem, Hanley, Longton and Tunstall became known as the Potteries. Apart from China clay, which mostly came from Cornwall, the potters needed fuel to fire the kilns and a plentiful supply of water. Both exist in great measure in the area and towns such as Kidsgrove and Newcastle-under-Lyme were to become centres of coal production. If the rapidly developing industries of the Potteries were to continue to flourish then the means to carry goods in bulk would need to be built.

A group of local industrialists formed the Trent and Mersey Navigation Company and called upon the services of the great pioneering canal builder, James Brindlay, to act as engineer for the construction of a canal linking the Trentside pottery towns with industrial Merseyside and the Midlands canal networks.

The problems facing Brindlay were enormous. The area is very hilly and the rocky sub-strata varies enormously. This is particularly so in the area between Alasger and Tunstall. Brindlay surmounted the hills by putting in two flights of locks and building the audacious 3000 yard long Harecastle Tunnel.

It was upon this second series of locks, climbing their way towards Harecastle, that Joan and I now looked from the warm and dry Red Bull lounge. A narrow boat had just entered a lock basin and Joan was fascinated to watch the teamwork required. One of the party leapt over the side, onto the bank, to operate the lock gates. Another team member prepared to climb up the ladder on the lock side to moor the boat. The helmsman at the rear was guided by another team member at the front as the delicate job of positioning the boat into the basin was undertaken.

Sitting in the comfort of the Red Bull pub, looking through the misted window, I wondered how our party would fare.

Through the mists of imagination I could see it all. Zoe would leap from the boat, confusing south with north, would jump from the opposite side to the bank and disappear into the oily black canal. Joan would scale the ladder but open the wrong sluices, drowning the boat in the adjacent basin. Andy, following my gesticulations, would steer the boat sideways into the lock, jamming it securely against the walls. Two hundred years of uninterrupted traffic would grind to an end as Brindlay's genius finally met its match.

I returned to my pint, dismissing all thoughts of a return journey by boat. Joan came in and as the draining water formed a puddle around her feet we discussed our next move. I rang Andy, asking him to meet us with tea and sandwiches on the A34 and after a few more minutes of getting dry we stepped out into the steady drizzle.

Andy and Zoe had reached our next camp site at Trentham gardens on the south side of Newcastle. In the comfort of the Red Bull lounge I deduced it would take Andy about thirty minutes to reach us. Forty-five minutes of plodding along the A34 and I was now getting concerned. No Andy. No shelter. Rain getting heavier. We plodded on. Fifteen minutes later a sign informed us we were only two miles from Newcastle and needing to turn left. The rain was creating monster puddles in our path. No Andy. Through the thickening gloom I made out the shape of another pub.

'Let's go in and ring Andy,' I shouted to Joan above the roar of the traffic.

We were just in time. As we raced for the door the rain came down in torrents. Streaming with water we burst through the doors of the welcoming … restaurant! It may have looked like a pub on the outside but it was certainly different on the inside. From the roar of the traffic to the roar of silence. All conversation ceased as startled diners stared. We stood sinking into the plush carpet, water streaming from our hair, down our Gortex anoraks and via our overtrousers themselves streaming with dirty brown water, flowed off dirty boots and into the surrounding carpet. A waiter, rehearsing any one of a thousand polite ways of saying 'Get out' came up to us. The rain was beating down outside, there was no way we were going back into that downpour. The waiter stopped six feet in front of us and stared, waiting for us to make the next move, hopefully out of the door. It was high noon in Newcastle. There was only one intelligent thing I could think of saying.

'A table for two please, and have you anywhere we can hang our coats?'

'Better than cheese sandwiches,' said Joan, reflecting on a recently demolished plate size steak. We had managed to make a three course meal last two hours and in that time the rain had eased. As we trudged into Newcastle I was contemplating the possibility of Joan and I being the only people to walk a thousand miles and put on weight. I had rung Andy, who was stuck in a Potteries traffic jam, and advised him of our new location, suggesting we meet later in the day as we no longer had a need for sandwiches. I looked at the map. We needed to follow the A34 into Newcastle but leave by the A519 Eccleshall road which would take us to Trentham Gardens and the camp site. Pretty simple really.

We reached a roundabout. I looked at the huge directional signs to see which way to go. I looked again at my map. I turned my back on the roundabout. I held my map upside down, back to front, I wanted to stand on my head. Whatever I did it was useless. According to the vast array of signs in front of me the A34 had ceased to exist, only to be replaced by Inner Relief Road. The A519 could be the one signposted by a black lorry symbol and labelled Alternative Route, or it could be any one of three indicated as leading to the M6. All five exits appeared to go to Stoke, one exit also said Town Centre. We followed that one.

Two roundabouts later and our confusion was total. Potteries road schemes were not designed for pedestrians. They were entirely devoted towards shunting black lorries along alternative routes to any one of three M6s or Stoke on Trent.

'Ask at the police station,' said Joan. I groaned, remembering Carlisle the previous year. I had no alternative. We made our way to the police station.

I stood at the desk, head reeling. A few minutes earlier I had explained to the lady policeman where we were hoping to get to.

'No problem,' she said. 'Leave here, turn left, at the toilets turn right, cross the road to the post office, keeping to the left of the post office go down the passage, take the second passage on the left, right by the side of a garage to the underpass, under that, over the crossing, through the supermarket car park, left at the gas works, first right, left in to Clayton Road and that is the A519 to Trentham'.

'Really,' I said, 'as simple as that,' convinced I would be walking around Newcastle for weeks until finally struck down by a black lorry looking for an M6.

We staggered out. Toilets, right, cross road — screech of brakes from taxi, post office-passage on left then second left — garage on right, gloomy underpass — interesting graffiti, Tesco's, gas works, traffic lights, road sign — 'A519 - Eccleshall', — whoops of joy as startled pedestrians avoid madman singing and dancing and throwing map in the air!

We reached the camp site in early evening. Cold, wet, sore feet from wearing boots and dejected at only managing eighteen miserable miles that day. The rain, which had never quite stopped, was again falling from the sky in sheets. Laundry facilities commonly found on camp sites were no match for the frequent changes of wet clothing we were having to get through. Every conceivable hanging space in the caravan and motor caravan was now draped with soggy socks, shirts, underwear. We ate our tea in sombre silence.

Andy, concerned that we may have had nothing to eat all day, had prepared a meal of gargantuan proportions. Unable to bring ourselves to telling him what we had substituted for the packed lunch, we struggled through. As we ate the rain eased. As we relaxed, trying to digest an overdose of food, watery sunshine replaced the clouds. As I slipped further and further into a wet pit of depression, evening sunshine sliced through the steamy caravan interior.

'Day's not over yet,' said Joan.

'I struggled to wake up, wondering what she was going on about. 'We've got time for a few more miles yet,' she said.

'I snapped awake. Looking at my watch, it was only seven o'clock, looking at the sky, clear and bright, looking at my map, Eccleshall twelve miles away. We both made a grab for trainers.

'Give you a ring when we get there,' we called behind us as we bundled out of the door.

It is amazing the change that can happen in two hours. Now, as we left Newcastle behind us, weak sunshine warmed our spirits. Wearing light trainers rather than boots was like floating on air. Birds singing instead of the constant roar of traffic was music to our ears. The weariness of the last few hours vanished as we skipped and joked our way to Eccleshall.

A few miles from Eccleshall and we came to the village of Swynnerton and the penal establishment of Drake's Hall.

'Pleasant looking place,' I said to Joan, surveying the modern, low level buildings, neatly planted shrubs and air of tranquillity. Joan had stopped at the entrance to the visitors' car park. At first I thought she might be seeking political asylum, anything to be free from the madman now stood behind her. Then I saw what had caught her attention. One of the neat little buildings to the left of the entrance had the word 'Laundry' written on it. One of the doors into this neat little building had the words 'Drying Room' written on it.

'We can't send Andy to the slammer just to get the washing done,' I said, but even as I finished saying it my mind went back to the view we had just left. Caravan and lorry, both resembling a Turkish bath, piles of unfinished laundry occupying every square inch of space.

'No we can't,' said Joan, heading off in determined fashion to the gatehouse.

We both arrived together, quite prepared to incarcerate Andy for the time it takes to dry fifteen pairs of socks. An imposing woman in blue uniform headed our way. I looked for signs and found the information I was dreading. It was a woman's prison. Getting him in might be a problem, getting him out would definitely be one. Resigned to wet socks we turned and once more headed for Eccleshall.

A little further on from Drake's Hall and we came to another establishment. Huge signs proclaimed it to be a military training camp. A picture of a Rottweiler surrounded by a red circle and signs saying 'No Entry' informed the casual passer by that Rottweilers were not allowed in. I wondered about humans but assumed that arriving without an invitation would probably lead to summary execution or, worse, being recruited into the military. Looking at the high walls and vast amounts of barbed wire I could only suppose that they had greater trouble keeping people in than the prison a little way down the road.

A few more miles and we reached Eccleshall and the welcoming fug of the Sun Inn lounge bar at about 9.40. We were elated. A day of damp depression had been turned into one of the best days so far. Thirty miles under the belt. Andy and Zoe turned up to help us celebrate. Over many pints of beer I plotted the following day's exertions, convinced we had turned the tide and the last of the rain was behind us.

At this point our plans were heavily influenced by the Department of Employment. Every fortnight Andy had to sign on as available for work. He had tried explaining that at all times he would be near a phone but the department were unyielding. Available for work meant being there, in person, at the benefit office. Andy had argued the common sense case that doing something for charity was better than doing nothing but common sense rarely has an impact with a career bureaucrat. By taking his holiday allowance Andy had been able to stretch his 'unavailability' to four weeks but two days' time was D-Day. He had to attend.

Heavily influenced by a well deserved intake of fine beer, I considered the logistics of the next few days. It was 17 June, day twenty-nine and we had covered 649 miles. We were two days ahead of schedule. We had arranged for two friends to take over for the days that Andy would not be available but in view of the opportunities for things to go wrong, I did not want them to be concerned with moving camp as well as acting as a support team. We were forty-five miles away from Kidderminster, two days' walking given reasonable weather, and the optimism generated by the amber nectar was convincing me of fine days ahead. We had not had a rest day since Stirling. Our laundry situation was desperate.

To an audience hanging on every word I made the first proclamation.

'We will have a day off when we get to Kidderminster,' I announced, followed by a further gigantic swallowing of fine ale.

Joan ordered more beer. She had been in need of a rest for a long while and was grateful for the mellowing effect that copious quantities of fluids were having.

I studied the map and camp site guide. Midway between Eccleshall and Kidderminster was the small, picturesque town of Bridgnorth. Just outside Bridgnorth was the Stanmore Hall bird gardens which boasted a camp site.

I made the next proclamation. 'We will camp for three days at Bridgnorth,' I announced to an enraptured audience.

Joan celebrated in fine style by ordering yet more beer. Not only a day off but a town to go shopping, sightseeing and eating in. I warmed to my admiring audience, now showing slight loss of balance and slopping beer, my beer, all over the place.

I proceeded to outline the logic of my grand design. Sipping from a dripping, half empty glass, I lubricated my throat. Joan lubricated the carpet by spilling Andy's beer.

'Tomorrow, in fine weather,' I said to an almost prostrate audience, 'Joan and I will walk to Albrighton, five miles from Bridgnorth. Andy and Zoe will take caravan and lorry to Stanmore Hall and meet with the relief team, Jacky and Phil, and show them the pick up point. Andy and Zoe will then return to Somerset, Andy to sign on and Zoe to process the pile of laundry.'

The thought of dry clothes was too much for Joan who ordered yet more beer.

I felt a rosy glow to my cheeks as I prattled on. 'The following day, Joan and I will walk from Albrighton to Kidderminster where we will meet Phil and Jacky and be taken back to Bridgnorth. Day three, Joan and I will have a rest day in Bridgnorth, Andy and Zoe will return with a pile of dry, crisp, clean laundry, Jacky and Phil will hand over the reins and we will all meet up that evening in Bridgnorth for a few pints.'

Brilliant! I looked at my slumbering audience. If they had only been awake to appreciate it.

The next morning I awoke to thundering rain and a thundering headache. The euphoria of the previous night quickly wore off as the thought of wet boots and wet clothes percolated my pickled brain. An ashen-faced Joan stirred beside me. 'At least the nice, fresh rain will clear our heads,' I tried to say cheerfully, ducking from a waterlogged boot flying towards me.

We were dropped off in steady drizzle by Andy and Zoe, who then continued to the next camp site at Stanmore Hall, just outside Bridgnorth. Fortunately our route was mostly along small, quiet roads through scenery that, if it was uninspiring, was at least quiet and flat. By the time we had covered ten miles and reached the small village of Gnosall Heath, the unpleasant effects of the night before had disappeared. We refreshed ourselves in a handy hostelry and trudged on. Eight miles and we were approaching Great Penyard Park along a very pleasant tree-lined avenue. The drizzle had turned to heavy rain and heavy rain was turning into a sustained pulse of a burst of heavy showers. Progress was now a dash from one tree shelter to another, wait ten minutes for the rain to ease, dash to another.

In this fashion we made a few more miles' progress and were only mildly saturated. Eventually we reached the hamlet of Tong, a mile outside the small town of Albrighton and within hearing distance of the M55 motorway that connects Telford with the M6 and the West Midlands conurbation.

Waiting for Jacky and Phil my mind went back to the previous year when we were a similar distance to Telford, but on the western side in Shropshire, convinced that the tide was turning and we could really get moving. Settling down to tinned curry and rice, one of Iain's more lavish attempts at cooking, I reached for the phone to book the next couple of camp sites. It was just before Easter.

'Sorry, booked up,' said the voice at the other end. Not too concerned I telephoned the next. Then the next. Twenty calls later I was convinced the world was spending Easter in Shropshire. We took two days off and visited Joan's mum instead.

Now, waiting for Phil, Jacky and more rain I was pleased that one consequence of our later start was that we were managing to avoid bank holidays. We were treated to a flying display by aircraft landing and taking off from the nearby Cosford RAF base. Phil and Jacky duly arrived just before an onslaught from the heavens and we returned to Stanmore Hall, having been able to tick off another twenty-one miles in uninspiring wet weather.

I listened to the knocking on the door. With a groan I looked at my watch. Half past six in the morning. I shouted some words that anyone with a working knowledge of Anglo-Saxon would interpret as 'Go Away'. The knocking persisted. I buried myself under the warm duvet. No escape. I could still hear it. I stumbled to the door and opened it. There in front of me, rattling tail feathers and displaying the most magnificent plumage, was a handsome peacock.

'Who is it?' murmured Joan.

'Lunch,' I replied maliciously, eyeing the plump breast and, at that unearthly time of the morning, a highly squeezable neck. I slammed the door and went back to bed. The knocking started again. Clearly he was not going to give up without his breakfast. I stumbled out of bed again and looked for something to give him. I picked up the carving knife, had second thoughts and picked up half a loaf of bread instead. I opened the door and threw it out. From out of a deserted sky swooped a huge cloud of ducks, geese and other exotic species. In seconds the loaf had disappeared. I threw out some old biscuits, oats, currants, muesli, rice, Rocky, still they kept coming. I searched in desperation, my imagination reproducing the sound that 4000 birds knocking on the door would make. With a flash of inspiration I hurled the contents of a tin of chicken curry out of the door. That did it. No self-respecting bird was going to hang around and be the next in the tin.

Two hours later we were trudging out of the camp site in dry but heavily overcast conditions. We skirted round Cosford air base at Albrighton and then headed vaguely towards the spa town of Kinver. Fourteen miles further on at the hamlet of Enville and it started to rain. For once luck was on our side and we had a handy pub to shelter in. An hour later the rain eased and we splashed our way to Kinver. Our route from there led through the Kingsford Country Park with its magnificent views from Kinver Edge overlooking the Severn Valley. We looked forward to this part of the walk. The only problem was finding it.

Arriving in the centre of Kinver, we came to a busy and complex five way junction. Logically we consulted the words on a nearby wrought iron, five finger signpost for directions to the Kidderminster road. We needn't have bothered. According to the post, if all roads lead to Rome, three of them do it via Kidderminster. I went into a nearby tobacconist to ask which of the three roads led to Kinver Edge and Kingsford Country Park. The very nice lady behind the counter explained that although she had lived in Kinver for nine years she had never visited the park and didn't have a clue where it was. A survey of all the customers in the shop produced an aggregate time of 129 years living in Kinver and of nine people who had never visited the park, five had not even been to Kidderminster. Convinced that I had been unknowingly beamed up by an extra-terrestrial spacecraft and deposited on another planet in a far off galaxy I rejoined Joan who was interrogating half the population of a local secondary school. They may have known what the capital of Botswana was and where to look in the sky for Ursa Major but they didn't have a clue as to the whereabouts of Kingsford or Kinver Edge. We set off, trusting to luck and the toss of a coin. A quarter mile up the road, round a bend and a huge spin proclaimed that we were in Kingsford Country Park..

We reached Kidderminster as drizzle started to fall. The nicest thing about Kidderminster is leaving it and we were grateful when Phil and Jacky arrived to take us back to the camp site and a day off in Bridgnorth.

Perched on top of a 200 foot cliff overlooking the River Severn, Bridgnorth is a lovely town. An interesting castle with magnificent views, a bustling main street with medieval archway, two small but interesting museums, there is something to interest everyone. We sauntered around, revelling in the relaxed atmosphere and a rest from the strain of worrying about the weather. Of course it rained but there are plenty of good pubs, cafés and restaurants to shelter in. We spent the morning sightseeing and shopping, the lunchtime eating and drinking, the afternoon sleeping and in the evening we celebrated the return of Andy and Zoe with more eating and drinking. One day may not have been enough to completely recharge batteries but we certainly felt the benefit the day after.

The following day we quickly left Kidderminster and soon reached the small Severnside hamlet of Holt Fleet, ten miles away. For the first time in days we had completely dry clothes to wear. Zoe and Andy were moving camp to Slimbridge, between Gloucester and Bristol, where we planned another three night stay. At Holt Fleet we stopped at the hostelry for lunch and a productive shake of the collecting tin.

Whilst avoiding where possible busy main roads, we had so far stopped short of walking on footpaths. There are a number of good reasons for this. Firstly, the existence of a dotted line on a map does not guarantee that a path actually exists. Whilst it is unlikely that a stretch of tarmac will be ploughed up between the printing of a map and our tentative footfall, it is quite possible the well-marked footpath on a map is in practice a ploughed field protected by barbed wire. Another good reason is that whilst a tarmac road has a predictable surface, a footpath could be anything from a boulder-strewn assault course to a British version of a mangrove swamp. The main reason, however, is the difficulty in route-finding often associated with cross country forays. It may be okay to spend a couple of hours retracing one's steps when on a Sunday afternoon ramble, it is another thing altogether when those extra miles and hours occur at the end of a long twenty to thirty mile day.

With these sensible considerations in mind, Joan and I chose to walk the next six miles using footpaths! We had not completely lost our marbles, although the euphoria of dry clothes at last may have had something to do with it. It was all down to logistics. The next twelve miles to Worcester were along a narrow, busy road without a footpath but with high enough hedges to conceal the endangered walker from the oncoming traffic. A network of what appeared to be well-marked footpaths not only avoided this hazard but also cut off a corner — saving three miles. As we were wearing boots we were not too concerned about conditions underfoot.

We left the comforting fug of our hostelry and after a hundred yards turned left to locate our path number one, which was to lead us to Holt Church. We were immediately confronted by two possible ways; one was tarmacked and led to a house, the other was a rough cart track which led through an open gateway into a field. We chose the latter. Ten minutes later, with the map orienteered to our chosen direction, I stood in the middle of what could have easily passed for a scene from a World War One movie. A rutted and broken field, ploughed almost to dust, stretched to the horizon in every direction and with no visible signs of a path. Mumbling something about another Ordnance Survey cock-up I retraced my steps. Joan was standing in someone's drive.

'I'm sure it's along here,' she said.

'I mumbled something about female stupidity and set off down the tarmacked path. Shortly before disappearing into someone's front living room the track veered right through a gate with a sign on it saying 'footpath'.

'Of course it's down here,' I said imperiously, 'but when navigating off the beaten track it's as well to explore all possibilities,' I said in my best Baden-Powell tone. Joan gave me that look that said 'My Hero' and followed on.

Half an hour later I was in the middle of someone's strawberry patch, trying my best to orientate myself with the map. The path had disappeared a few yards before.

'If only I had a compass,' I said, in my best Ernest Shackleton tone.

'If only you knew how to use one,' Joan mumbled.

I finally percieved what appeared to be a faint path setting off in the right direction and, stepping gingerly over strawberry plants, started to follow it.

Twenty minutes later we had reached a stream at what was probably the only impassable point.

'If only I can find a large branch,' I said in my best Edmund Hillary voice, scouring the undergrowth.

Joan appeared on the other side of the stream just as I was about to wade waist deep across. Teetering on the brink of oblivion I just managed to avoid falling in head first.

'How did you get there?' I said.

'I used the bridge,' she said, indicating a lesser path leading to an obvious bridge fifty yards upstream.

Half an hour later we were nearing the end of our epic journey. A hundred yards away civilisation in the form of the village of Hallow Heath beckoned. Between the welcoming embrace of the houses and people and the wilderness we had traversed stood a wall topped with barbed wire.

'If only I had a ladder,' I said in my best Chris Bonnington voice.

I gingerly placed my coat over the barbed wire. Both hands on top of the wall, a hop and both feet joining my hands. Tottering, chest against the barbed wire, bum sticking in the air, what the hell do I do next.

'Let me give you a hand,' said Joan, appearing on the other side.

That did it. With a sobbing cry I slowly rolled backwards into a patch of nettles.

'Try using the gate just around the corner,' said Joan, in her best Queen Victoria, not-being-amused voice.

'Never again,' I said to Joan, as we walked along the main road into Worcester. 'You could have injured yourself,' I said, the rain cooling off the nettle stings on my legs and arms, washing the wire cuts clean, rinsing the mud out of my hair.

Joan gave me another 'My Hero' look.

Worcester is one of those county towns that could be called typically English. It has a beautiful cathedral, a beautiful river bank, people playing cricket and gentle folk eating strawberries with footmarks on them. It also had men from Severn Trent Water Authority flushing six inch water mains clean, causing torrents of crystal clear water to gush through roadside hydrants. Seeing hundreds of gallons of fresh water pouring out of those huge hydrants was was too much for two tired and thirsty walkers.

'Can we have a drink?' Joan asked, meaning, 'can you lend us a cup of water?'

The man backed off. He looked at me, covered from head to foot in mud, scratched and bleeding, strawberry leaves stuck to boots, an apparition that could have come straight from a 'Hound of the Baskervilles' movie.

'Help yourself,' he stammered, backing away and indicating the torrent gushing out of a six inch main.

'Have you got anything we can drink out of?' Joan asked.

The man pretended not to hear. There was nothing else we could do. We knelt down either side of the hydrant, mouths inches away from the torrent.

'Just paying homage to Hydrant, the goddess of water,' I said to a passer by, who hurried on muttering something about working too hard and needing a holiday. On the count of three we plunged our faces into the glistening flood. Beautiful. Nectar. Refreshed we stood up, water dripping off faces, waved to the gathering crowd of startled onlookers and made our way into Worcester.

As we crossed over the River Severn the sun came out. The park-like banks of the river, with the cathedral as a backdrop, is a particularly beautiful sylvan scene which went to our heads. We had intended finishing for the day, but not wishing to waste sunshine considered walking further. We found a dingily lit wine bar and spread the map over a greasy table whilst drinking revolting coffee. In the background a Pink Floyd record was being gently played at 120 decibels. I looked at our proposed route, following the west bank of the Severn along a narrow B road to the small town of Upton-upon-Severn.

'We could always follow the East Bank,' I said, indicating a footpath that stuck to the bank.

Joan had run out of 'My Hero' looks and instead gave me a 'You're a Genius' look.

'Of course, this path would be a lot easier to follow,' I said to Joan, 'we just stick to the river bank.'

There it was again, that 'You're a Genius' look.

We drank our coffee. I rang Zoe and told her to meet us at Kempsey, a small village on the banks of the Severn about five and a half miles away. Leaving Pink Floyd to reverberate around the wine bar we stepped into warm evening sunshine. As we walked along the hard-surfaced tow path that leads out of Worcester we both opted to walk in shorts and removed our tracksuit bottoms.

The hard surface gave way to a muddy track as we left Worcester behind. The path climbed steeply up and then traversed a steep, muddy slope before disappearing into woods carpeted with a mass of damp looking undergrowth. As we reached the woods all semblance of a level path ceased and we found ourselves crossing a muddy slope that fell steeply into the river. The next half mile was a desperate lurch from one tree trunk to another, boots skidding on the greasy surface. Eventually the path levelled out and we came into open fields. Open, that is, except for waist-high, man-eating stinging nettles. The decision to walk in shorts now rebounded on us as we waded barelegged through the nettles. Struggling to stand stork-like on one foot whilst trying to roll tracksuit bottoms over the other foot threatened to pitch us headfirst into the fiery undergrowth. Nowhere safe to sit down, no option but to grit teeth and plough on.

The path ceased along with the nettles. A rusty barbed wire fence barred progress. We paraded up and down but could find neither stile nor gate. To our left a quarter of a mile walk to a road, to our right the River Severn. No option but to go over the rusty wire. We put out coats over the top strand and gently and then desperately straddled over. A path continued the other side only to open out in a camp site with the usual 'Private, No Entry, Trespassers will be Caught, Shot and Fed to Crocodiles' warning notice. It was too late in the day to take any notice. We crossed the camp site, Joan smiling sweetly at who we thought may be the owner, me trying to remember the name of a good lawyer. Footpath the other side, more nettles, private slipway, more fences and then, Kempsey Church. We made our way to the front of the church and duly waited for a late-arriving Zoe.

As we drove back to the camp site I reflected on the day and for the fifth time made a vow to always stick to tarmac. We had made over twenty-five miles that day. Spreading the map out I was relieved to see that the rest of the way to Upton-upon-Severn and unification with our planned route was mostly on quiet stretches of tarmac.

The following day dawned bright and sunny. With buoyant spirits we returned to Kempsey and giving a cheerful wave to Zoe set off for Upton-upon-Severn, ten miles away. We duly reached there just before noon and enjoyed delicious coffee and cakes in the Marina Café. Opening out the map to appraise myself of our intended route, I was attacked by that sinking feeling. Six months previously, when planning this route in the warmth and comfort of my Somerset home, I had been attracted by a series of bridle paths and footpaths that threaded their way over the M6 motorway and around the private Bredon School.

We left the marina in bright sunshine and after threading our way through Upton-upon-Severn we turned left off the busy main road onto some blissfully quiet roads to the small hamlet of Queenhill. To my immense relief the first part of our 'off road' route was well marked and well signposted. By now the clouds were gathering and I was mindful of the weather forecast that predicted the possibility of thundery showers. The bridle track crossed the motorway and then entered the grounds of Bredon School, where a helpful sign invited us to turn left into an open field. The clouds grew blacker. I can take most forms of weather but I die at the thought of lightning.

In 1967 I gained membership of the lucky strike club by being blasted off a cliff face I was climbing in the Lake District by a bolt from the blue. I was told the odds of being involved in a lightning strike were seven million to one. Anxious to emulate the feat, in 1990, returning home from Manchester, my car was nearly blasted off the road by a lightning bolt. I was told the odds of a double lightning strike were forty million to one. Any comfort I got that I had been stupendously lucky was dispelled by Joan who reminded be that things happen in threes and as 'HE' has missed twice I shouldn't count on a bad aim three times in a row.

As we dutifully turned left into the open field the path disappeared. I heard a distant rumble of thunder. The clouds grew blacker.

'Come on,' I said to Joan who, with impeccable timing wanted to do some sightseeing. I walked quickly in what I hoped was the right direction. Another distant rumble convinced me I should not be too concerned about the laws of trespass at this point. We made our way to the Strictly Out of Bounds driveway.

Rain started to fall as we left the school grounds the posh way. We walked faster. The rain became heavier. The thunder got nearer. The rain reached torrential proportions. We were only wearing trainers and soon these were saturated. Just as the rest of our clothing threatened to disintegrate in the downpour an open barn came into view. We made a dash and reached shelter just as a downpour became a deluge, whatever the difference may be.

For the next hour we helplessly watched the rain. I passed away the time wondering how the weatherman would describe this lot. As pulses go this was a heavy one but as it was becoming continuous could it be called a burst of heavy pulses becoming continuous as heavy showers gave way to a more sustained band of rain, thundery in places? Eventually it eased and we made our way along roads streaming with water to the tiny and picturesque village of Forthampton. I rang Andy and arranged to meet him at the village of Town Street four miles further on. Andy was concerned that we might have been caught out in the downpour/deluge but I told him of our fortuitous shelter and that the rain was now easing.

With saturated feet and virtually saturated everything else we left Forthampton. Everywhere was streaming with water. Avoiding ankle deep puddles was impossible but our feet were so soaked it did not matter. One mile out of Forthampton the torrents started again. This time there was no shelter. With the warm sunshine earlier in the day we had opted to wear our lightweight waterproof tracksuits. They were no match for this weather. The water began to stream in through every seam, every zip. There was no escape. Totally saturated, in torrential rain, we met Andy at Town Street and returned to the camp site. It was a sombre group that ate their way through curried peacock that night. The weather forecast gave no comfort that the heavy rain would ease. Once again we were losing the laundry battle. we had walked twenty one miles that day. Good for the conditions but not good if we hoped to keep ahead of schedule.

I opened my eyes and listened to the familiar sound of rain beating off the roof. The weather forecast was rarely wrong when predicting lousy weather and as another day dawned I could only think, 'right again!'

I awoke my partner and we dressed for battle. Joan and I were in determined mood. We had no idea how long this weather would last so we had no alternative but to do battle with the elements. Boots replaced trainers, heavy waterproofs replaced tracksuits. Andy took us to Town Street and we set off in steady rain. Eight miles further on and the rain intensified. It was Sunday. As we walked past row after row of terraced houses through the outskirts of Gloucester I began to think of 'normal' people. People sitting down to Sunday lunch; people sitting round nice warm fires, oblivious to the wild, stormy weather outside; people to whom the definition of madness was going for a walk in this weather. Joan was also hallucinating. She was beginning to imagine that the streets were running with gravy, that the peppermints in her pocket were really roast beef. With this dramatic decline in our mental states we reached Gloucester Docks and met with Andy.

Andy took us to a café near the cathedral. They were really pleased to see us. We hung our wet clothing on the hat stand, thus ensuring every other coat sharing the stand would be as wet as ours by the time we had finished. With an ever increasing pool of water gathering from our dripping coats, we sat our dripping bodies down at a table. As the water ran off our heads, down our bodies, over our boots, small pools of water gathered at our feet. Over coffee we discussed the next move.

Joan and I now had the bit between our teeth. We were going to achieve our target for the day even if we had to swim the rest. Our route took us six miles out of Gloucester to the Sharpness Canal, then along the towpath for eight miles to Slimbridge and the camp site. We arranged to meet Andy again at Hardwicke Farm, just before leaving tarmac for the towpath. Refreshed we got up to go, splashing our way through a now waterlogged carpet to a coat stand threatening to float away in the ever increasing lake rising over its feet. With fortified determination we then set off into the downpour.

Navigation can sometimes be a problem in heavy rain. Take the map out of its waterproof cover and it soon disintegrates into sloppy lumps. We were in a new housing estate and no one had told ordnance survey of its existence. I looked around to where houses had replaced fields, lamp-posts had replaced trees and roads had replaced footpaths. I had no choice but to unfold my map and by revolving around in ever decreasing circles I managed to orientate myself to what I thought was the right direction. As my map dissolved I decided on the way ahead.

Trusting more to luck than judgement we set off past rows of neat semi-detached houses. I looked at the last shreds of map in front of me just in time to see Gloucester dissolve under the weight of another forty blobs of rain. With no map we trusted to memory and it was with relief that I saw signs pointing to Hardwicke Farm, our meeting spot with Andy.

Eight miles later we met him armed with a flask of steaming coffee. By now even our Goretex-proofed 'heavy weather gear' was yielding to the elements. Ten minutes of shelter in the Land Rover, welcome mouthfuls of Andy's coffee and two distinctly damp people bade farewell and started off along the towpath.

It's nice to know, when faced with serious questions over one's sanity, that we were only beginners in the madness stakes. On this cold, wet, windy Sunday the banks of the Sharpness Canal were lined with dozens of people doing nothing else but watching the canal fill up! Dozens of them, sitting there under a variety of umbrellas, watching the raindrops make pretty patterns on the water! They were anglers. Listening to the language I assumed they were coarse anglers. Judging by the looks on some of the wet, miserable faces, the fish had more sense than to come to the surface only to get brained by thunderous drops of water falling on their heads.

'You must be mad,' said one big game hunter, 'going for a walk in this weather.'

'At least I'm keeping warm,' I explained to another fisherman whose huge rod threatened to reach the other side of the bank. The writing on his jacket told us he was from Bolton. We told him we had walked through Horwich, the sister town to Bolton.

'What, today?' he replied, incredulously.

I explained that on wet days we restricted our walks to below a hundred miles and had in fact started the day from just the other side of Gloucester. He explained that this was a heat of a major fishing competition. Somehow 'heat' seemed the wrong word in those conditions. It was one of those days when five pounds of fish would win everything. Joan offered to nip back to the fish market in Gloucester and get a few cod steaks but they declined our offer. With cheerful wishes expressed on both sides we left the banter and repartee behind us and continued on our way.

As afternoon cloud turned to evening gloom we reached Slimbridge and the camp site. Even though we were saturated, Joan and I expressed quiet satisfaction. In probably the worst weather conditions encountered so far, we had walked twenty-three and a half miles.

We hung our wet 'heavies' next to our wet 'lightweights' from the day before. The weatherman was talking about the rain stopping tonight and tomorrow remaining mostly dry when some more rain would come in from the west during late afternoon. Tactics for tomorrow were simple. Trainers and lightweights till lunchtime. Meet with Zoe and change into heavies for the afternoon. Then we hoped to reach Bristol and what for us would be home territory.

Home Ground

It was 24 June. Day Thirty-Five and 767 miles under the belt. Our plan, agreed the previous night, was to walk as fast and as far as possible in our lightweights, while Zoe and Andy moved camp to Edithmead, near Burnham on Sea, sixty-five miles away. We were not over the moon that in these desperate weather conditions our back up team would be so far away but Edithmead was a crucial location. Whilst being at best three days walk away, it was easily and quickly reached by a fast dash down the M5. Most importantly, it was only twenty miles away from our home and would allow our house to be used as an emergency laundry. Yet again the inability to dry clothes quickly was causing acute problems. We estimated that Andy and Zoe could establish camp at Edithmead before lunchtime and then return to meet us on route so that we could change into our 'heavies' well before the forecast deluge.

We wanted an early start and at half past eight we were ready. As a precautionary check I placed a call through to the Bristol Met. Office who confirmed that a heavy band of rain, moving eastwards, would reach the region by mid-afternoon but until then it would remain dry. The BBC weather forecast was saying similar things so we felt reasonably confident of a good start.

Even though it had stopped raining at six o'clock the previous night, such was the volume of rain that had fallen, huge puddles still covered the narrow roads that we were to follow for the next six miles. It would require very deft footwork if we were to keep our trainer-clad feet dry.

Slimbridge is the home of the Wildfowl Trust founded by Peter Scott. It is based on the mudflats of the Severn Estuary and is one of the premier bird sanctuaries in Europe. The surrounding area is part of the flat Severn tidal plain, rich if wet farmland. As we left the camp site a heavy mist covered the flat land all around. The silence was eerie. Nearby is the obsolete Berkeley Magnox nuclear power station. Pylons marching from the soon to be dismantled generator loomed out of the mist. Cries of birds echoed through the still air. I had a great sense of foreboding.

Despite the wet conditions under foot we were going well and by nine o'clock were over two miles from the camp site. A drop of rain spattered in my face. Joan also felt rain. 'Condensation,' I said, with no real conviction. 'In this mist water would be dripping off everything.'

As if to counter my flimsy theory another drop of rain rebounded off my nose.

'It's raining,' said Joan.

'Rubbish!' I said, as two drops competed for the privilege of bouncing off my head.

Ten minutes later we were in no doubt. Not only was it raining but it was beginning to rain quite heavily.

Five more minutes and in desperation we were grouped over a soggy map.

'Too late to go back,' I said. 'They're on their way to Edithmead by now,' I concluded, referring to our efficient back up team who would be away from Slimbridge in the time it would take to return. Joan sensibly suggested we cancel our stroll along country lanes and make for the A38, a busy trunk road, where there would at least be cafés and pubs to shelter in.

Our shortest distance to the A38 was three and a half miles and in determined fashion we set off. The rain was coming down even harder when out of the gloom loomed the shape of a telephone box. Joan and I crammed ourselves into it's welcoming confines and I telephoned for the cavalry. At least I tried to. The telephone wouldn't accept any money. It wouldn't register any response to my frantic button pressing. It just sat there and purred. I cursed Sod and his stupid law. All the way from Land's End to John o'Groats, then from Dunnet Head to Gloucester we had been pleasantly surprised by the quality of British Telecom's public call boxes. Now in our moment of greatest need we came across the first duff one!

We left the box and continued towards the A38. The rain was now equalling the downpour of the previous day. Our trainers were offering no resistance to the deluge. Our lightweights, still damp from two days earlier, were beginning to resemble sieves.

We reached the A38. Our spirits rose. A hundred yards in the direction of Bristol there was a public call box. Almost opposite, in a lay-by was a Portakabin bearing the magic inscription Café. We stumbled into the café completely saturated. Joan ordered bacon sandwiches and large cups of tea whilst I went to the telephone box across the road.

It was a highly relieved and highly wet walker that opened the door of that box. I didn't care about the water that seemed to gush out. All I wanted to do was contact base and get someone out to us before we caught pneumonia. The rain was coming down in sheets and it was still early morning! I dialled the number. Nothing happened. I changed coins. It simply went in one end and and came out the other! The unthinkable gradually dawned on my waterlogged brain. Sod was having a real good day. This phone didn't work either! I could, however, dial the operator. With cold fingers I dialled 100 and listened to the ringing tones.

The operator was a long time answering and I couldn't help noticing the roof leaked directly above my head. To pile on the misery the box was beginning to fill with water and I was standing ankle deep in a puddle. The operator answered. I requested a transfer charge call to a mobile phone.

'Cannot do that,' said the operator, 'we have no way of recharging transfer calls when they are made to a mobile phone.'

I searched desperately for inner patience and calm. I explained my predicament, how we were walking for charity; how we were stranded with waterlogged lightweight clothes and a back up team sixty miles away; how, now we were nearing home territory, an awful lot of publicity would be coming our way and surely he would like Telecom to be seen in a charitable light. Another leak in the roof was hitting the handset, splashing into my mouth as I spoke. The operator was intransigent.

'Nothing I can do,' he said, 'however, you can try speaking to the supervisor.'

I searched for more inner calm. I opened the door to let out some water. The supervisor came onto the line and I closed the door as the water receded to below ankle level. I patiently explained the story again.

'Let me see what I can do,' said the supervisor, 'I will come back to you in a minute.'

Five minutes later I opened the door again to reduce the water level to below the plimsoll line. I was now beginning to shiver violently with cold. The torrent from the roof was finding gaps in my clothes I never knew existed. I hung on for what seemed an eternity. More leaks appeared in the roof, the latest one finding the gap between hood and neck and sending a cascade down my back. Finally the supervisor came back on the line.

'Cannot do anything,' he said.

I searched for more inner calm but a 'Sorry Empty' sign appeared in my eyes. I explained I had an urgent appointment for a radio interview, BBC TV would probably want me on the six o'clock news and I couldn't keep Wogan waiting.

'I'll see what I can do,' he said and disappeared for five more minutes. I opened the door to let water out, I shifted positions in the shower cubicle, I marvelled at a handset that still worked when waterlogged.

'Can't help you,' said the voice, 'the only thing you can do is to ring someone reverse charges and ask them to pass a message on.'

Inner calm was replaced by core meltdown. I enlightened the man as to my views on British Telecom. I enlightened the man on our dire situation. I explained that people walking from John o' Groats to Land's End do not carry a Filofax and unfortunately my personal computer would not fit in the rucksack. I explained it was his phone that didn't work, a BT mobile phone I was trying to contact and the network was BT-owned Cellnet.

He listened impassively. When the mushroom cloud was finally settling he replied, 'I'm sorry to hear you're a bit upset, but unfortunately rules are rules.'

As I returned to the café, Joan was just collecting hot bacon sandwiches. I related my dismal tale. The café owner suggested I try a garage 200 yards down the road. I trudged out and made for the brightly lit canopy shining out of the gloom.

With dismay I heard the manager explain they no longer had a public phone. With elation I heard him offer the use of their private phone if it was a local call. With dismay I heard him say that a call to a mobile phone did not qualify as a local call. A lady cleaning toilets came out and complained about the pool of water collecting at my feet. The manager indicated with an air of impatience that I should really leave and let him get on serving his non-existent customers.

I trudged back to a cold bacon sandwich. An imaginary cloud of depression began to appear over my head, matching the real clouds outside. My waterlogged brain could neither remember handy telephone numbers nor handy people guaranteed to be around to answer the desperate ringing of a phone. Traffic outside splashed past, creating bow waves, washing tides of black muddy water against the Portakabin. A bus went past. A brightly coloured bus operated by my ex-colleagues.

'Why don't you ring Trevor's secretary at their head office?' said Joan impassively, referring to the super efficient secretary to the company chairman. I choked on a greasy bit of cold bacon. What a brilliant idea.

I returned to the smouldering telephone box. A tide of dirty water washed over my feet as I opened the door. I redialled the operator. I asked him to ring the only number I could be guaranteed to remember regardless of circumstances. I heard him ask a voice at the other end if they would accept a reverse charge call from the Stroud area. With everything crossed I heard the voice at the other end finally agree. Then I was put through to Joy, my ex-boss's secretary. I felt as though I had rediscovered a lost civilisation. Joy was the epitome of calm, professional efficiency. She took down the details, promised to phone Andy and make sure he understood them, said if she could not get hold of Andy she would make sure someone would come out and pick us up.

It was with lighter heart I went back to the cold tea and sandwiches. I knew I could rely competely on Joy and I was greatly relieved that on a day that saw the widest repertoire of Sod's laws, we were fortunately on home territory with help close to hand. An hour later Andy turned up with a Land Rover full of dry clothes. We got changed and trudged another eight miles along the A38. The roar of traffic was amplified by the wet conditions and spray from passing lorries was adding to the heavenly torrent making visibility almost impossible. The good news was that thoughtfully a footpath had been provided along the edge of the A38 so we were at least seperated from the traffic, an important consideration in the sort of murky weather we were walking through. The bad news was it did not appear to have been maintained for about a thousand years and we were constantly having to wade through waist-high wet grass, tripping over potholes and avoiding souvenirs left by the packs of wild dogs that obviously judging by the volume, roamed these parts.

We trudged on, ears tuned for the sound of howling wolves. We heard only the roar of howling diesels. The rain and noise were incessant. In a convenient car park fronting an office block we met Andy. We had had enough. After sixteen miles we gave up and returned to the camp site. This round was won by the weather.

That night, in dismal silence, we watched the weatherman on television explain what went wrong, how a deepening low had sudenly accelerated, sweeping up the western approaches faster than expected and gathering moisture all the time, which it then kindly dropped on my head. On this miserable day the weatherman chose to announce that we were walking through the wettest June for 362 years. I would have hated to do this walk in 1629.

The following morning we climbed into clothes that for once were pleasantly dry. We had hoped to be starting from the south of Bristol today but the events of the previous day had put paid to the grand plan. With depressed spirits we sat in the Land Rover as Andy sped us north along the M5, past Bristol, and to our finishing point the day before. At the small town of Thornbury, on the busy A38 a few miles north of Bristol, we climbed out and surveyed the dry but glowering sky. A brisk, cold wind was carrying the damp portents of another miserable day. Digging deep into the last remnants of morale we trudged off in damp boots along the unattractive, noisy road towards Bristol.

Eight miles later, head aching from the noise of heavy traffic, spirits sinking as more rain descended from cold grey skies, we reached the outskirts of Bristol at the suburb of Cribbs Causeway, an appropriately noisy junction between a hugely busy dual carriageway going into the heart of the city and the M5 motorway.

We had arranged a meet with Zoe just off Cribbs Causeway at an obvious junction on the map. Once again what looked good on the map was totally different when translated into urban streets. Arriving at the 'unmistakeable' junction I was horrified to see traffic cones stretching to the horizon in every possible direction. Bright yellow signs announced Road Closed (the road we was meeting on), Diversion (the road Zoe ended upon) and

No Entry (the road we were on).

We searched desperately for a phone box and found one outside a school. A couple of rings and a loud Antipodean voice cut through the crackle.

'Where are you,' I asked.

'Lost,' was the reply.

'Lost where?' I asked.

'Lost, parked outside a school,' was the reply.

'What school?' I asked.

'Dunno,' was the reply, 'but they wear black blazers, grey skirts and trousers, green and black ties and the school badge is a gold, blue and red crest, and the brats seem all to be about fourteen years of age and smoking.'

I had a mental picture of Zoe holding two 'brats' hostage in a smoke-filled Land Rover whilst she graphically described what they were wearing. I sent Joan into a child-filled chip shop to see if the uniforms matched. They did. We rang Zoe back, told her the uniforms matched, she must be outside the same school and if she drove round the block we should eventually meet.

Two minutes later our Land Rover emerged at sixty miles an hour from a side street, scattering chip-eating, fag-smoking crowds of local youth everywhere. Inside the Land Rover were more dry clothes, hot tea and sandwiches that I was sure I saw being made a couple of days ago. Zoe had got lost in the maze of urban side streets but for once her innate direction finding pointed her in the right way. Sensibly finding an easily identified landmark she had parked up and waited for the inevitable phone call. Eating my way through a tough cheese sandwich I considered the rest of our planned day.

From Cribbs Causeway our route threaded through surburban streets around the western fringes of Bristol to the junction with the M5 at a point where a spectacular bridge carries the motorway in a flying leap over the River Avon. Thoughtful road builders in the 1970s had included a cycleway and footbridge in the construction and this was to be our means of crossing the river, thus allowing us to avoid the busy city centre of Bristol. Leaving the motorway footbridge at a point near Gordano Services, progress southwards would be on quiet country roads skirting the southern 'dormer' villages of Bristol.

We left Zoe and the warmth of the Land Rover and trudged off in drizzling rain, having arranged to meet up again at

Gordano Services. In blustery wet conditions we reached the junction with the M5 and it was with some disquiet I pondered on the next one and a half miles of aerial walkway as the road soars 200 feet above the River Avon. The bridge shuddered with the weight of the thundering traffic as we steadily climbed towards the summit. Despite the wind tugging at our anoraks and the vertiginous drop to the river below my apprehension was unjustified. The spectacular views of the Avon Estuary, the Bristol Channel curving around the Clevedon Bay and the distant views of the lofty headland of Brean Down, the southern boundary of Weston Bay, more than made up for the unpleasantness of the immediate surroundings.

We descended towards Gordano Services, leaving the motorway about one and a half miles before that welcome stopping point. Two miles of urban street through the riverside suburb of Pill and we were in the risky business of walking into the service station car park, easy game for the stream of traffic competing for space on the entry road.

We had walked sixteen miles by the time we met Zoe for the second time. Despite the intermittent rain we had remained reasonably dry even if that meant uncomfortable walking in boots and 'heavies'. I desperately wanted to be well south of Bristol by the day's end. Six more miles would see us into the dormer town of Nailsea and less than thirty miles from the camp site at Edithmead.

Marching towards the steamed up Land Rover I could dimly make out the shape of Zoe holding aloft a flask of steaming brew and a handful of cheese sandwiches. My jaw still ached from the encounter earlier with the lead-lined lunch. My nose still twitched from the acrid reek of the smoke-filled covered wagon. I looked at Joan who gave me a 'You Must Be Joking' look before marching off to the cheery confines of the services cafeteria.

With the map spread out over two tables I selected a rendezvous point that I was sure Zoe could not miss. As the main road from Gordano enters Nailsea there is a steep hill and sharp bend before entering the modern urban sprawl.

'Anywhere between the bend and the town centre,' I said confidently to Zoe, indicating about fifteen miles of highway.

Both Zoe and Joan gave me 'You're So Masterful' looks. Zoe was adamant she couldn't miss. Joan stocked up with enough food to see us through the night on the grounds that anything was possible. We refreshed ourselves with fresh coffee before marching on to an uncertain rendezvous in Nailsea.

Four hundred yards from Gordano Services we were able to leave busy main roads for quiet side lanes that led to the pleasant village of Portbury. Watery sunshine was breaking through grey clouds, always a morale booster. A few more miles and we were forced to join the busy, winding road that led to Nailsea. The road started to descend steeply and with everything crossed we approached the sharp bend in front of us. Rounding the bend and there was Zoe, parked just off the road but sufficiently protruding to cause a tailback of respectable proportions. Zoe didn't care. Enough had gone wrong today as it was without continuing further and possibly making a rendezvous more difficult. It was seven o'clock at night when we climbed into the Land Rover, having made our apologies to forty irate drivers and shaken our box at forty more.

That night we returned to Edithmead beneath an ominous sky, but dry, having achieved twenty-two miles and with Bristol truly behind us. A visit by some friends made a further contribution to our feeling of optimism. Over many pints we regaled our friends with the story so far and it was a cheerful group of people that retired for the night shortly before the arrival of morning!

I opened my eyes with trepidation. Only a few hours earlier I had eventually got to bed, having celebrated probably to an excess. The expected retribution did not happen. I felt tired but no hangover, no thunderous headache.

'Could this be a good sign?' I wondered. Something else was different. Slowly, as senses returned to an anaesthetized nervous system I realised what it was. There was no sound of rain bouncing off the lorry roof; instead there was sunshine streaming through the window. Joan groaned as I let my enthusiasm for the new day be widely known. Slowly she emerged from the cocoon of our duvet.

'What's the forecast?' she said, disbelief all over her face as she looked at the sunlight streaming through the window.

'Forty per cent risk of showers, getting better the further south we get,' I replied, having already made the decision what to wear.

The damp boots were put to one side, the waterproof 'heavies' left hanging on the line. Today was going to be a day for lightweights. This close to the camp site, this close to home, it was worth the risk.

It was in buoyant mood that we arrived back at Nailsea and the pick up point from the night before. Hurriedly we packed the rucksack as Zoe parked the Land Rover rear end into the oncoming stream of traffic. We looked forward to the day ahead in a new mood of optimism. With a cheerful wave we said goodbye to Zoe, the Land Rover and fifteen fuming drivers as we set off under a blue sky. The black clouds of the last few days were now replaced with white puff balls, the sun warm and comforting.

Nailsea is a clone of the standard new town to be found near every big city in England. Surrounded by pleasant countryside, row upon row of semi-detached houses, quiet street after quiet street, all looking the same. It did not take us long to get hopelessly lost. Just as desperation was beginning to creep in we saw a sign that said Town Centre. We had originally planned to avoid this part of town but now the necessity of knowing exactly where we were overcame all aesthetic considerations. We reached the anonymous rows of shops, anonymous covered precinct and much needed anonymous public conveniences that pass for a town centre just as the sun disappeared behind a cloud slightly greyer and slightly larger than the others in the sky. We found a café, had a cup of coffee with a map spread all over the table, asked thirty-five people the way before finding someone who seemed to have a working knowledge of the Nailsea geography, and set off again.

Our misgivings about the weather disappeared as we emerged into warm sunshine, the ominous cloud having passed over. We left Nailsea and threaded our way along some beautifully quiet country roads. After the roar of motorways, urban through routes and major dual carriageways that had been our constant companion for the last few days, the next ten miles were a blissful haven. Every so often the blue sky would disappear behind a veil of cloud but nothing happened and the clouds passed over. After ten miles we were in the small Mendip village of Congresbury, straddling the main A 370 trunk road that connects Weston-Super-Mare with Bristol. This was truly home territory, the South West, the final laps. We were going well. A most pleasant cup of tea in Congresbury, a few more miles and we reached the traffic-choked village of banwell.

Just outside this village there is a 150 year-old castle, built originally as a mansion house but eccentrically designed as a replica Norman fortress. The castle stands in twelve acres of grounds, the main feature of which is a 350 year-old Mulberry tree planted in the reign of James I. I couldn't help thinking it might have been planted in 1629 as the June rains flooded the ground and the *'Court Chronicler'* recounted that it was the wettest June since Christendom began. To help meet the enormous costs of upkeep of the castle, the present owners have turned part of it into a hotel and café, and it was in these palatial surroundinsgs that we next stopped for food and refreshments.

'Twenty more yards and we will be in Somerset,' I said to Joan as a crumbly piece of delicious scone, overburdened with jam and cream fell into my lap. Neither Joan nor I are born West Country people, though we have a great deal of affection for our adopted county. I was born in London but in my late teens left home to live in the industrial North West mostly to be near the cliffs and mountains of North Wales and the Lake District and to indulge myself more frequently in my passion for rock climbing. It was there that I met Joan, my children were born in Oldham and for the next few years we settled in the Manchester district.

Then came British Leyland. It was 1976 when I joined this ailing giant as a junior finance manager at the Truck and Bus head office near Preston. A year after moving house to the Preston area I was asked to perform a rescue attempt on a small subsidiary company in London and it was to the South East we moved as I took up a new position as financial controller of the troubled subsidiary. Two years later I was asked to do the same again, this time on a larger and much more important subsidiary in Bristol. This was our first visit to the West Country and we soon found out what a delightful place Somerset is. We lived in a small Mendip village thirteen miles south of Bristol and enjoyed a quality of life that we didn't believe possible after living in Manchester and the South East.

It was not to last. Three years later I was appointed general manager of a new venture that involved setting up a nationwide network of parts and services centres to support the bus industry, a market that British Leyland dominated. This involved moving back to the head office of the bus division based in Leyland, near Preston. We moved to a house just outside Lancaster, in the glorious Lune Valley and whilst continuing with a high quality rural lifestyle we still missed the unique charm of Somerset.

In 1986 my involvement with the bus industry put me in contact with a group of people working for the National Bus Company. This state-owned giant was shortly to be broken into sixty pieces and sold off as part of the government's continuing programme of privatisation. This particular group of highly capable people wanted to buy the bit that they worked for, the provider of country and urban services in the Bristol area and based in the seaside resort of Weston-Super-Mare. They possessed all the skills necessary to run a highly successful bus company but were short of a finance director. The Gang of Four asked me would I like to be the fifth and it took me three and a half minutes to make the most important decision of my life. A year later we had bought the company, had got off to a flying start and that year Joan and I moved back to Somerset, to a rural location between Bridgwater and Taunton.

Now, as we sat twenty yards from the Somerset border, I pondered on what a unique place it is. Most people who pass through Somerset do so at high speed along the M5, on their way to the holiday resorts of Devon and Cornwall. Few realise what jewels they are speeding past. The first jewel the southbound traveller comes to is the Mendip hills. A designated area of outstanding natural beauty, this range of limestone hills runs east to west, from the beautiful city of Wells in the east to an abrupt fall into the Bristol Channel at Brean Down in the west. The most notable spot in the Mendips is the great limestone canyon of Cheddar Gorge.

Leaving the Mendips behind, the M5 motorway now skirts the western edge of the Somerset Levels. This designated area of special scientific interest is the largest low level moorland in Great Britain. Beautifully quiet, carpeted with lush green grass, these wetlands are the home of many unique varieties of flora and fauna. It also has a chequered history. At the eastern edge of the Levels is the town of Glastonbury and its conical shaped tor. When the Levels were covered by sea and salt marsh, the tor was an island, the Isle of Avalon and reputedly the home of the mystical King Arthur. The Levels also became the home of another king for it was here that King Alfred escaped from the clutches of the Vikings and sheltered before subsequently raising his army and marching off to eventual victory.

In 1685 the bastard son of Charles II, The Duke of Monmouth, raised an army to contest the reign of James II. Just outside the small village of Westonzoyland, about six miles east of Bridgwater, the two armies clashed and Monmouth was defeated. This rebellion, named the Pitchfork Rebellion after the West Country farmers who formed the rump of Monmouths' army, culminated in the last battle on English soil. Retribution for the people of Somerset and Devon was severe. Judge Jeffries established his 'Bloody Assize' in the Great Hall in Taunton and hundreds of men and families were executed, deported or suffered brutally as they served long jail sentences of hard labour.

To the west, south of Bridgwater, rises the Quantock Hills. This ridge of old sandstone was the first part of England to be designated an area of outstanding natural beauty. Home to one of the largest concentrations of wild red deer in England, the wooded coombes that cut into the sides of the ridge are areas of peaceful, tranquil beauty.

Now, as one passes the county town of Taunton and approaches the small town of Wellington, the Blackdown Hills rise to the left. These hills form the southern boundary of the Levels and also form the border with Devon. To the right rises the final jewel, again shared with Devon, and this is the Exmoor National Park. At the north-western edge of Exmoor sits the coastal resort of Minehead.

Somerset is not only blessed with geographic charm. The uplands of Exmoor and the Quantocks protect the county from the wilder ravages of the prevailing westerly weather and the climate in the county tends to be warmer and drier than in the surrounding region. Speculating on this climate I could not help noticing that the sky was now clear of cloud and the temperature had noticeably risen. We finished our cream tea and stepped out into warm sunshine. Twenty yards later, on blissfully quiet roads, we walked into Somerset. Around a bend and off came tracksuit trousers and tops and for what seemed to be the first time for a very long time we walked in shorts and tee shirts.

The scenery also changed. Near the twin hamlets of Christon and Loxton a beautiful panorama opened out and we found ourselves looking down the full length of the Loxton Valley to Bridgwater, twenty miles away. We had walked over twenty miles so far and now, approaching a telephone box in the middle of nowhere, we decided it was time to arrange a meeting with our back up team. There was an obvious location to meet at. Four years ago, when it became obvious that our company was going to grow into something quite big, the chairman and I took the decision to move the group head office away from the operational centres, thus allowing managers the opportunity to run their bits of the business without the impediment of having senior management breathing down their necks. In looking for a new head office we wanted something quite small, thus ensuring that the head office staff remained small, and also quite rural to provide a quality working environment. We bought a disused farmhouse between Bridgwater and Weston-Super-Mare, only two miles from the motorway junction at Edithmead, and christened it Badger Manor in honour of the smiling badger logo that adorned all the company's products and rolling stock. It was to that location, five miles away, that we now headed, arriving at six o'clock at night.

The meeting with Andy went smoothly and we returned to the camp site only two miles away. How fortunes had changed! The last few days of torrential rain, days when twenty miles was a struggle, days when cold and wet dampened spirits, now seemed light years away. We had achieved twenty-six miles that day, 26 June. We had walked in warm sunshine, no rain, the first dry day since 7 June. On the day that we reached Somerset it had been the first dry day for twenty days. I thought about the following morning, when hopefully we would pass through Bridgwater, pass within half a mile of home, and pass through Taunton. We had to run a proverbial gauntlet, but a pleasant one of ex-colleagues, friends and well-wishers and an interested and supportive local press. It was going to be a long day and a busy one. In jubilant spirits we turned in for an early night to prepare for the rigours.

We did not have far to walk for our first meeting the following day. Dropped off by Andy at Badger Manor, we walked through the door and made our way to the chairman's office. Trevor and all my ex-colleagues had been so supportive of our fund raising efforts that they were by far the biggest contributors to the collection. We were greeted by Joy who had passed on our message of desperation a few days earlier. Then Trevor and the rest appeared and over many cups of coffee we told them the story so far. Half an hour later, with cheerful farewells, we set off back to the camp site, two miles south and on our route.

A few days previously we had given out a tentative timetable to various people that envisaged our arrival in Bridgwater early in the morning. However the recent rain had slowed us down, that morning's meeting at Badger Manor had been scheduled for the previous night and we did not now envisage reaching Bridgwater until about two o'clock. We left Zoe and Andy to notify others of our revised timetable and to move camp further up the road to Wellington, and set off. The weather was warm when we left the camp site and we were again wearing shorts.

Our route was straightforward. Straight down the A38, through Highbridge to Bridgwater, then on to our home town of North Petherton before leaving the major road for quiet, minor roads to Taunton.

Ten miles further on, in perfect weather, and we were on the outskirts of Bridgwater. A little way up the road a car had pulled to a halt and a man carrying a punnet of strawberries came walking towards us. As he came nearer I recognised the familiar face of a photographer from a local paper. We had planned to meet this particular media baron at a strawberry farm between Bridgwater and Taunton, but our revised timetable now envisaged not being there till five o'clock.

'Got to be somewhere else by then,' said the beaming media man, 'we'll have to take the photographs here.'

'Here' was a downtown dusty street in urban Bridgwater opposite a DIY superstore, not quite the rural strawberry farm nestling in the fold of the Quantocks. Clutching his punnet of strawberries the inventive photographer paraded up and down until he found what he was looking for. 'This will do,' he said, indicating someone's front garden.

We marched up to the low brick wall boundary of the garden.

'You sit on the wall and we will use the garden as a background, pretending it's a strawberry farm,' he said.

We stared in amazement at this substitute for a strawberry farm but assuming all these media people are really wayward artistic genii we played ball. Sitting on the wall we adopted a variety of poses, clutching strawberry punnet, feeding each other strawberries, picking strawberries magically from a wilting crop of exhaust-stained wall flowers.

The free goon show was too much for the passing motorists.

First the traffic slowed, then stopped altogether as a mad pair of yellow-shirted walkers picked strawberries from a front garden whilst a beserk photographer used up fifteen rolls of film to capture the magic moments. Eventually the photocall was over and we were free to continue on our way, assurances ringing in our ears that the readership of this particular newspaper would not be able to tell the difference between a 200 acre strawberry farm and the front garden of 212 Bristol Road.

A little while later we were in the centre of Bridgwater and approaching the closed down and dilapidated ex-technical college. A car screeched to a halt in front of us and two people dived out. I recognised one of them as the photographer with another local paper. His associate was carrying two beer glasses and a bottle of amber liquid.

'Meant to meet you at the Walnut Tree this morning,' said the manic photographer, 'but can't wait till this afternoon,' he concluded. 'Have to take the picture here,' he said with a global sweep of his arm that encompassed most of Bridgwater. His eyes lit upon the abandoned shell of the technical college, in particular at the overgrown lawns on one side. 'This will do,' he said, leaping over the wall and disappearing into the undergrowth.

We followed lamely, wondering how this mess could possibly take on the appearance of North Petherton's up-market hotel.

'We will pretend this is the Walnut Tree's beer garden,' said the photographer.

I mumbled something about my favourite watering hole not having a beer garden but it fell on deaf ears. I could only watch in disbelief as the man and his friend proceeded to make an overgrown grassy bank look like a neatly manicured lawn by leaping up and down on the waist high grass, squashing it flat. Numbly we sat on the appointed spot and adopted a variety of poses featuring two glasses, bottle of beer, bare and blistered feet and happy grins surrounded by waist high grass. Eventually another photocall was over and we continued on our way with assurances that the readership of yet another paper would be completely fooled, this time into believing that an overgrown, rubbish-strewn grassy bank was really a non-existent beer garden in a prominent local hotel.

Four miles later we were on the outskirts of North Petherton when a car screeched to a halt in front of us. I looked at our immediate surroundings and wondered how another enterprising

part of the local media circus would persuade their readership
that a motorway roundabout was really a beer garden in the
middle of a strawberry farm, or a strawberry farm in the middle
of a hotel, but my fears were groundless. It was a reporter
wanting to know if we had seen two long distance walkers
wearing bright yellow shirts. I gave him a few minutes to focus
his vision on our bright yellow shirts before introducing ourselves
and giving an interview, happily without photographs.

We marched on in beautiful weather. A clear blue sky and
warm sunshine. Eventually we reached the Walnut Tree in
North Petherton and a stop for a well-earned drink. With the
good wishes of many friends ringing in our ears we left the
Walnut Tree and continued up the A38 to the strawberry farm
at Thurloxton. Another stop, real strawberries to eat, and on
again. This time we left the A38 and disappeared down some
quiet backroads, passing within half a mile of home.

The previous year we had planned a route that, by means
of a long easterly loop, bypassed our house by about twenty
miles. Our reasoning was that by the time we had reached that
part of Somerset we would have walked about 200 miles; the
reality of what we were doing and going to have to do would
just be sinking in and we didn't want to be tempted to give up
by passing so close to our home. This year we could afford to
be much closer. With 850 miles gone and only 200 to go there
was no temptation.

We eventually reached the Bridgwater canal and followed the
towpath to eventually reach Taunton at six o'clock. It had been
a magnificent day; we were reluctant to end it there, so a call
was made to Zoe in Wellington to tell them that we intended
to carry on until eight o'clock and could they set off then and
meet us on route. After a brief refreshment break in Taunton
we set off again. Finally, at Sawyers Hill, just outside
Wellington, we were met by Andy and Zoe. It had been a
memorable day. Beautiful weather, a lot of interest and thirty-
two miles walked. Tired but elated we listened to the weatherman
explain the presence of a ridge of high pressure, further cold
fronts in the Atlantic, but a promise of fine weather tomorrow.
With keen anticipation we turned in and had no problem
sleeping that night.

Early morning sun filled the lorry as Joan and I made
preparations for another day's walking in warm sunshine. Andy

dropped us off at our starting point just outside Wellington which we quickly left behind. It was most pleasant walking, blissfully quiet roads and a cloudless sky. The terrain was now getting much hillier. Uninformed opinion usually believes that the most rugged walking is in Scotland. This is not so. In Scotland roads tend to follow lines of least resistance, valley bottoms, etc. and gradients are fairly civilised. The worst terrain is in Devon and Cornwall where the big lumps of Exmoor, Dartmoor and Bodmin Moor give little room for manoeuvre and where road builders seem to have delighted in meeting the terrain head on. Roads go over hills rather than around them, fall into valleys at the steepest point and cross moorlands at the bleakest and most exposed points.

Eleven miles into the day and we crossed into Devon at Westleigh, near Tiverton. It was with some sadness we left Somerset, the only English county we managed to walk through and keep dry! Eight miles further on we reached Tiverton, a welcome café and a meeting with Andy to discuss the next stage of the day. The weather was glorious and Joan and I were now feeling quite fit. Despite the increasing ruggedness of the terrain we felt good for a lot more miles yet. I also wanted to ensure that we got close enough to reach Okehampton the following day, as this would give us an ideal location to move camp to. A look at the map confirmed that from now on the route was on isolated, quiet roads, the weather was ideal and the scenery breathtaking. We agreed to meet Andy seven miles further on at the small hamlet of Templeton Bridge.

Leaving Tiverton we were amused to see the name of the road was Longdrag Hill. Two miles further on we were appreciating how the road came to be so named. Panting and wheezing we finally reached the crest of the hill 780 feet higher than when we started. The road now followed a high ridge with the Exe Valley on one side and Exmoor on the other. This was delightful walking.

A few more miles later we reached a regional speciality near Templeton Bridge. The infant River Dart at this point carves a deep cleft through the soft soil and rock bed. The road, unable to follow the contours around this obstacle, instead chooses to fall headlong into it. Passing signs warning of dire consequences to anyone daft enough to drive a car into this miniature grand canyon, we walked, and then as the gradient steepened, we ran to finally meet the bridge at the bottom. What goes down must go up and fifteen minutes later two panting, wheezing and staggering walkers finally crested the steep slope that climbs out of this dark ravine. At the top we met Andy, now refreshed and recovered from an arduous drive down and then up.

'Thought you might need a drink,' he said with overwhelming understatement.

I took the opportunity to look at the map. Despite the recent exertions we were still going well. A natural stopping point was at the small village of Black Dog, six miles away. Refreshed we sent Andy on to Black Dog and set off with buoyant spirits, enjoying warm evening sunshine.

We reached Black Dog after more marvellous walking and were driven back for what seemed an enormous distance to the camp site at Wellington. That evening it was all jubilation. We had walked thirty-three miles that day. In three dry days we had walked ninety miles and from a seemingly never ending proximity to Bristol we were now well into Devon and possibly into Cornwall in two days' time.

Final Steps

It was 28 of June, 896 miles walked, 170 miles to go, and it was with an air of jubilant optimism that we left the camp site in Wellington for the last time. Andy was taking us to our start point at Black Dog, caravan in tow behind the Land Rover, before moving on to the next camp site at Bridestowe, four miles south of Okehampton. I was looking at the map and speculating on the opportunity of getting past that north Dartmoor town twenty-two miles away. In this region the terrain can make a mockery of distance but we were both feeling fit, relatively free of injuries and the weather forecast was promising. The attacks of neuralgia had receded both in intensity and frequency since leaving the Midlands and with less dependancy on drugs the excrutiating bouts of cramp were also becoming less frequent.

Andy duly dropped us off at Black Dog and we agreed that probably the next time we would be in touch would be when we got close to Okehampton.

Devon is a most blessed county. A fine coastline with many sandy beaches, rugged headlands, moors and hills, green pastureland. What makes Devon so special, though, is the ever changing, gently rolling countryside at its heart. Neat, picturesque villages nestling in folds of lush, green hills. Our next eighteen miles was through some of the best countryside Devon could offer and whilst the rolling terrain made for strenuous walking, there were many picturesque pubs to find refreshment in, many quiet village greens to rest on, pleasant, friendly people urging us on with kind thoughts and good wishes. As we walked through this ever changing kaleidoscope the great brown hump began to dominate the forward view. This huge upland of Dartmoor has a mixed reputation.Famous for its prison, built to house French prisoners during the Napoleonic Wars, the reputation is one of brooding isolation. Any reader of Conan Doyle's *The Hound of the Baskervilles* would consider the moor to be an eerie and mysterious place. For the solitary walker the moor is one of the last great wildernesses, a place of solitude and peace.

Many outdoor groups and military training units use the moor. Last year we followed a route that took us from Tavistock to Okehampton along the very edge of the open grassland. We stopped for a break at a café and Joan got into conversation with some people camping across the road.

'Scouts?' Joan enquired.

The man spluttered, sending bits of sausage roll around the room. I noticed a green beret. Trying to drop a hint to Joan I started talking about green-headed men. Joan almost got the hint.

'Ah, your cub leaders,' Joan said, as half a platoon of Royal Marine Commandos prepared to introduce themselves. Not wishing to hang about and discuss this insult to their unit, I left, dragging Joan behind me just as she was about to ask whether they were only trainee cub leaders.

This year our route was to pass the north of that desolate and windswept moor. Four miles from Okehampton and avoiding military units like the plague, we reached the small village of Belstone Corner and stopped at a handy telephone box to ring our ever alert back up team.

'Hello,' said the voice at the other end.

'It's me,' I cried through the crackle of static.

'Hello,' said the voice at the other end.

'Speak to me!' I yelled, the static now reaching deafening proportions.

'Hello,' said the voice at the other end.

I expected to get the time. 'At the third hello the time will be . . .' but no, all I got was a continuous tone indicating that contact with the civilised world was lost.

'Not to worry,' I said jauntily, 'if they know we can't get through they'll move the phone to somewhere where they can get a better reception. Let's walk on and stop at the next call box.'

'Hello,' said the voice at the other end.

'Can you hear me?' I shouted, futilely as the next thing I heard was that continuous tone again. We had walked for two more miles towards Okehampton and stopped at another call box.

'Not to worry,' I said jauntily, 'if they know we can't get through they'll come looking for us. Let's walk on and we'll probably meet them on the way.'

We reached Okehampton. I found a phone box, went in and dialled the magic number.

'Sorry, caller, the number you have dialled is unobtainable,' said a female computer with a voice like a Dalek.

I stared uselessly at the handset. I thought of all possible things that could have gone wrong. Last year, when trying urgently to reach Iain to tell him of an enforced change of plan, I got a similar message. We walked four miles back to where the lorry was parked to find that he hadn't switched the phone on! Of course. That must be it. 'Don't worry,' I said jauntily, 'they must be on their way and switched the phone off to save battery power.'

It started to rain. We made for a nearby hotel which was technically closed. With typical Devon hospitality the hotelier listened to our plight and allowed us to shelter from the rain and use the public phone in the hotel. I tried to ring again, had a pleasant conversation with a female android and rejoined Joan.

'Let's find a café, have a drink and then wait on the bridge to meet them,' I said jauntily.

We had a drink of coffee. In pouring rain we waited on the bridge in the centre of Okehampton that carries the main road from Bridestowe and would be the only way Andy and Zoe could get into Okehampton. We had another drink of coffee. I looked at the map. Whilst the camp site was only four miles away it was in the opposite direction to the way we wanted to leave Okehampton and would be a wasted four mile walk in pouring rain. We really needed to make contact with our back up team. I went back out in the pouring rain, waited on the bridge, returned like a drowned rat.

'You try ringing them up,' I said to Joan, less than jauntily.

Joan went to the phone box. Two minutes later she returned. 'Don't worry,' she said jauntily, 'I've rung for a taxi!'

Half and hour later we arrived ignominuously at the camp site, courtesy of a friendly taxi driver.

'I don't know what could have gone wrong,' wailed Zoe, 'the

signal indicators all looked good.'

I picked up the telephone. It was indicating a strong signal reception. I tried dialing a number. All I could get was a tone telling me I had insufficient power to send or receive. I plugged the thing into the mains. No good. With a sinking feeling it dawned on me that we were now the proud possesors of a malfunctioning and virtually useless telephone. Over dinner we discussed contingency plans. The best we could think of was to ensure that at any time we would be unlikely to want to walk to the camp site, Zoe or Andy would have to stick close by in the Land Rover. It was a messy, time-consuming and boring job for whoever was driving the Land Rover but we could see no alternative.

We were joined that evening by our other son, Steven, who insisted on buying us dinner at a local hostelry. Arriving at the appointed place I lent Steven the money to buy dinner whilst I retrieved a collecting tin from the Land Rover.

Joan and I always took a tin with us but being shy about rattling it under people's noses, we tended to leave it perched prominently on the end of our table. Steven did not share our shyness. As he went to the bar to order dinner he took the tin with him, vigorously shaking it under people's noses and pointedly referring to the two middle-aged charity walkers 'sat over there'.

Two hours later, having successfully borrowed more money so that he could buy me a drink, he went to the bar and took the tin with him, vigorously shaking it under people's noses and pointedly referring to the two elderly charity walkers 'sat over there'.

A fine evening came to an end. We got up to go. Steven insisted on one for the road. Resignedly I gave him the money to save him borrowing it. He went to the bar and took the tin with him. Resignedly the remaining customers coughed up whilst he pointedly referred to the two geriatric charity walkers 'sat over there'.

After a wet night, a wet day. In pouring rain we returned to Okehampton. It was back to boots and 'heavies'. We marched out of Okehampton on a busy road in poor visibility but the courteous drivers of Devon were more than careful to give us a wide berth, protecting us from the worst of traffic spray. Two miles outside of Okehampton we turned onto a very narrow and very quiet road that in a few miles would take us to the small village of Bratton Clovelly.

The road climbed steeply and then levelled out onto a plateau which gave good views of the road in front. I could see the familiar blue outline of a milk tanker, stationary and completely blocking the road. As we got closer we could see that there was a car, also stationary, barring further progress for the tanker.

The car was one of those of Eastern European origin that is the butt of many jokes. The driver of the milk tanker had his head in the boot, which was at the front, whilst smoke poured from the engine, which was at the rear. Two ladies, jabbering away in a language I took to be Italian, were explaining, in excited fashion, to cows, open fields and trees what had gone wrong. A tractor, unable to make progress, had stopped behind the milk tanker and the driver came ambling over as we reached the car.

'Small engine,' I said, talking about the boot at the front that had nothing in it except the tanker driver's head. The head eased out of the boot and explained that the cooling system appeared to go all the way round the car, from the engine at the back, to the boot at the front. Another car pulled up behind the tractor and the occupants came ambling over. More excited wailing, this time to the heavens, hands held beseechingly towards a weeping sky, proclaimed to the assembled multitude that this was too embarrassing for words.

The latest arrivals came over and having dispensed a couple of the statutory jokes about Skodas proceeded knowledgably to dive into the engine compartment. The tractor driver's head disappeared into the boot.

'Start 'er up,' a voice said, as another new arrival dispensed another variety of Skoda jokes. The engine burst into life and smoke erupted from the back, completely enveloping six heads that were in the engine compartment.

'Turn 'er off,' said one of the three heads that were in the boot.

'What goes faster than a Skoda?' said another new arrival as more black smoke mushroomed out of the bonnet.

With the cabaret getting a bit stale we edged our way past the row of cars and the milk tanker, that by now was probably a yoghurt tanker, and carried on our way.

A few miles later, in incessantly heavy rain, we neared the village of Bratton Clovelly where Andy or Zoe would be waiting. There another regional speciality waited for us.

In fact it was difficult to read the name of the village on the map due to the quantity of black arrows that adorned all the roads, indicating steep gradients. Before plunging into the bowels of the earth I looked back down the road from whence we came. A ribbon of cars led to the spot where another puff of black smoke rose lazily into the sky.

As we fell headlong into another tree-lined ravine it was difficult to believe this was the easy way into the village. As we puffed, wheezed and groaned our way out we cursed the inflexible boots on our feet which made walking up a steep gradient an ankle twisting affair. We reached daylight, Bratton Clovelly and Andy all at once. The rain was easing and the temperature was noticeably warmer, adding significantly to the unpleasantness of grinding up steep slopes wearing a heavy anorak.

Andy poured tea out of a flask whilst I looked at the map. The next eleven miles to Launceston, the ancient capital of Cornwall, was on pleasantly quiet roads of moderate terrain. The sky was clearing, even patches of blue sky were shyly peeking out from rain heavy clouds. We changed into our lightweight tracksuits and trainers and having made arrangements to meet Andy at Liftondown seven miles away we set off, leaving him with an empty flask and a pile of wet clothes.

In emerging sunshine we walked on, our elevated position giving outstanding views of the surrounding countryside. First past the recently constructed Roadford reservoir, then across the valley to the unusually named village of Broadwoodwidger. Normally I look at my map frequently in countryside like this, identifying places of interest, but today I was relying mostly on memory as my map had become saturated in the morning's rain.

We came to the elevated crossroads of Rexon Cross and headed for the hamlet of Lower Cookworthy and Launceston. We came to another crossroads and I tentatively opened my map, waterlogged bits falling off it and splits appearing along the creases as I did so. I looked at the road layout in front of me and again looked at my map.

'If we are at Lower Cookworthy then someone had better tell Ordnance Survey they have got their map wrong,' I said confidently to Joan.

I am proud of my map-reading skills. Many years of

navigating over harsh mountainous wilderness and through isolated and wild areas have honed my ability to read maps to a fine edge. If I can't relate map to terrain then it must be the map's fault. I looked again. I looked at other parts of the map. The awful truth punctured my confident arrogance. Two miles earlier, at Rexon Cross, I had taken the wrong road. Not only was my error adding more miles to the route, the extra miles would be along the hideously busy and narrow A30 trunk road.

If the air was grey that morning it was blue that afternoon as we trudged downhill to meet the A30 two miles north of Lifton and six miles north of Launceston. Everything was to blame. My arrogance, stupid traffic departments for erecting stupid signposts at stupid crossroads, Joan for not telling me to check my map at Rexon Cross, Andy for not possessing divine sixth sense and coming back to tell us we were going wrong. My mood did not improve as we reached the A30 and were greeted by the deafening roar of traffic. Into the village of Liftondown we marched, my foul mood deteriorating by the minute, by now blaming the Prime Minister, Archbishop of Canterbury and Roland the Rat.

As we walked through Liftondown we were stopped by a little elderly lady out for a walk with her granddaughter. I was blaming lack of papal insight for our misfortune as she questioned Joan about the logo on our shirts. Realising it was a Sunday I was about to lay the blame firmly at the door of the rest of divinity as she reached into her purse and produced £2. 'Put that into your box,' she said, just as I was moving on to blaming other cosmic lifeforms.

Brought back to Earth I explained our collection box was left behind at the camp.

'You wouldn't be doing this if you weren't honest people,' she replied. 'Take the money and put it in the box when you get back to camp.'

My return to Earth was made absolute by the lovely, unsolicited kindness of this lady. As we left her and her granddaughter I realised the world wasn't so bad after all, that we really had not gone far out of our way and if it hadn't been for my intuitive foresight in taking the wrong, sorry, alternative road we wouldn't have met such a nice lady and our funds would be £2 worse off!

We met Andy at Liftondown. Holding aloft two tins of cold

beer he explained about his equally satisfying afternoon. Casting around for a café to refill the flasks, he could find none and opted to knock speculatively at a house. On hearing the story the owner was delighted to help out by refilling the flasks with boiling water and as Andy was leaving dived headfirst into a large fridge, emerging with an armful of cold beer as an offering for two presumably thirsty walkers. This was a fitting end to the kindness and hospitality we had experienced in Devon. Leaving Andy with two empty beer cans we marched on, into Cornwall and another meeting at Launceston, where we regrouped.

It was now early evening and we had managed twenty-two miles plus a bit more for my inspired act of genius in taking the wrong, sorry, deliberately alternative road. The next few miles were along a busy dual carriageway stretch of the A30. I did not fancy walking that on a busy Monday morning and a quiet Sunday evening was ideal. Five more miles, the worst stretch out of the way, we called it a day. Twenty-seven miles of mixed weather, mixed fortunes and ultimately huge gestures of kindness had given us a day to be well pleased with.

The next morning Andy dropped us off at our start point before continuing with the caravan to our next camp site at Bodmin. We agreed to meet at Bolventor, at the famous Jamaica Inn, the subject of the Daphne Du Maurier novel of the same name. The first three and a half miles of our planned route were on quiet lanes but the next three and a half miles were on another busy stretch of the A30. I was not looking forward to it and it was with mixed feelings that we found roadworks extending along the length we should have been walking. The road was being widened to a dual carriageway and all the traffic being diverted onto the old road whilst a new section was built alongside.

As far as the eye could see there were heavy plant, steaming tarmac, men in hard hats and keep out signs. I looked at Joan. Joan looked at me with that blissful smile I remembered so well from the Dornoch Firth. Two great minds thought alike. With unseeing eyes we skirted round one Keep Out sign, weaved past a gigantic tarmac layer, smiled blissfully at startled road builders. With nimble feet we skipped over steaming tarmac, climbed over oil drum barriers, smiled blissfully at more hard-hatted people. With Jamaica Inn appearing in view we quickened our pace, broadened our smiles and left footprints in setting concrete. With a final flourish, a victory roll vault over a crash barrier, we arrived at Jamaica Inn, having avoided three and a half miles of traffic-choked road.

Once again the weather was deteriorating as we set off again along the narrow road skirting Bodmin Moor and circumnavigating the marshy reservoir at Colliford. It was Zoe's turn to drive ahead and wait and four and a half miles past Jamaica Inn we met again at Colliford Down. Although the weather was changeable, we were quite confident that the next ten miles to the camp site would not pose any great problems and we let Zoe off from any more boring chaperone duties to return to the camp site. The next few miles consisted of quite steep undulating terrain but we were rewarded by fine views from traffic-free roads.

With twenty miles under the belt so far that day we met up again with the A38. Our route lay to the left but the camp site was half a mile to the right. We were both feeling fit and wanted to continue. There was a phone box on the road junction and with crossed fingers I tried the magic number. It was our lucky day. We were rewarded with an Australian voice coming over loud and clear. We told Zoe that rather than return to the camp site we would be carrying on and we gave her a location five miles further on to meet at.

From this point the scenery changed dramatically. Leaving the wild open views of Bodmin moor behind we approached the lunarscape of the St Austell area. China clay has been excavated from this area for centuries but with the birth of the industrial revolution the demand rose dramatically and to be able to meet this demand the excavations had to be enlarged on a mechanised grand scale. We walked past towering white spoil heaps, gaping holes in the ground, eerily abandoned workings. Fittingly, in this Armageddon moonscape the sky clouded over and heavy rain began to fall. Workings, rusty with age, loomed out of the mist, rivulets of white rainwater ran in the gutters.

We reached the village of Mena and met with Zoe. The rain eased and we opted to walk another three miles to put this moonscape behind us. We left Zoe and shortly after there was a deluge. At the village of Bugle, twenty-eight miles from the day's start point, wet and cold, we met Zoe again and returned to the camp site. We now seemed to be progressing in large bounds and the deteriorating weather was no longer the depressing influence that it had been in the past.

The next day we set off from Bugle in murky weather whilst Andy and Zoe continued to Chacewater, near Truro, and the next camp site. We continued walking through moonscapes, through the divinely named villages of St Dennis and St Stephen, where we met with Zoe. It was raining steadily but not sufficient to seriously trouble our lightweight waterproofs. A drink and a sandwich and we agreed to meet again ten miles further on at St Erme.

The rain appeared to be lessening by the time we duly reached our meeting point. We had made twenty miles so far and were clearly benefitting from being able to wear trainers and lightweight clothes. Zoe had turned into Andy and we agreed to meet next at the village of Shortslansend, five miles further on and five miles from the camp site.

Waving goodbye to Andy we set off on an isolated narrow road, down the statutory steep hill into a tree-lined cleft and an equally steep ascent up the other side. As we disappeared into the cleft the sky darkened. Ominous heavy drops began to fall. A rumble of thunder, the rain getting heavier. Desperately we looked for shelter. The rain became torrential, the road a stream of muddy water, steep banks either side releasing lumps of earth loosened by the rain. As another clap of thunder echoed through the sky we heard another rumble, of a diesel engine. I dared not hope, then round a bend, lights blazing, came the fifth cavalry, or at least Andy in the Land Rover.

We clambered into the warmth and shelter of our motorised covered wagon just in time. For the next hour we watched the storm rage from its protective confines. Andy had just reached the meeting point when the sky darkened. Mindful that we were clad only in our lightweights he had the presence of mind to trace our route on the map and then come looking for us.

After an hour the storm began to pass over and the rain eased. Clambering out we set off again for Shortlanesend as our haven disappeared in a cloud of spray. Two miles later we met again. We had achieved twenty-four miles that day, the weather was deteriorating again and the camp site was five miles away. Good reasons for stopping but Joan and I were in determined mood. We were so close to our ultimate goal that we felt unstoppable. After a drink and a snack we said goodbye to Andy and set off for the camp site. An hour and a half later we splashed in, soaked through but satisfied with a day when over twenty-nine miles had been walked through atrocious conditions. Lizard Point was now only thirty-three miles away, at most two days, walking.

The next day we left Andy and Zoe to move camp to Marazion whilst we set off towards Helston. We had agreed that we would try to telephone when we reached Helston but we also had a contingency plan to meet at a crossroads at two o'clock if we had not been heard from.

From the moonscapes of St Austell we were now walking through the ghost towns of Cornwall's tin mining past. Ruined engine houses, chimneys leaning over at crazy angles, grass-covered spoil heaps, all around were testaments of Cornwall's once great tin mining industry.

As we passed another ruined engine house I could not help thinking of another Cornish great, the engineer Richard Trevithick. If James Watt claimed to have invented the steam engine, if the firm of Boulton and Watt held the first patents, it was Richard Trevithick who first made steam work.

Flooding had always been a problem with the deep Cornish mines and all sorts of weird contraptions were used to pump them dry. It was as a young engineer that Trevithick, realising the potential power of steam, first harnessed it as the motive power for a crude reciprocating pump. The applications were vast, the performance, even with those early prototypes, so advanced that Trevithick's engines came into great demand. From workshops in Hayle and Cambourne Trevithick produced ever bigger, ever more efficient Cornish beam engines for use throughout the world. Some of those early engines were even in use throughout the first part of the twentieth century.

Trevithick did not stop there. He could see the ultimate application of the power of steam. From his engineering genius and his working knowledge of harnessed steam power came, in 1808, the world's first steam locomotive. Sixteen years before *Locomotion* rumbled along the Stockton and Darlington Railway, twenty-three years before the *Rocket* won the Rainhill trials, thirty-seven years before the *North Star* ran from Bristol to London along Brunel's mighty broad gauge, Richard Trevithick's steam locomotive *Catch Me As You Can* demonstrated the potential of steam power to a sceptical world audience. From one extreme part of the country to another, Trevithick steam-pumped mines dry. In the Northumberland coal mines Cornish beam engines not only kept the mines dry. Cornish locomotives running on wooden rails provided some of the haulage power. The potential of steam did not escape the notice of a young Geordie engine house assistant called George Stephenson.

Twenty miles after leaving Chacewater we reached the town of Helston. Our route to Land's End now went off in a south-westerly direction around Mounts Bay to Penzance. However, before we could rejoin that route we had another appointment at Lizard Point. The early rain had eased and again we felt unstoppable. After a brief rest we made the decision to carry on to Lizard Point, thirteen miles away. We found a phone box, again the gods were with us, and having got through to Zoe we made arrangements to meet at a point just south of Culdrose Royal Naval Air Station. From there Zoe would be walking with us to Lizard Point, leaving Andy in the Land Rover as support.

We reached the high security perimeter fence of Culdrose at around two o'clock. Half a mile further on, just past the heavily guarded main entrance, we were passed by the familiar shape of our Land Rover, Zoe at the wheel. Zoe, coming from North Queensland, is not familiar with security at British miilitary bases. Seeing us she abandoned any idea of driving on to the prearranged meeting place and pulled up hard against the security fence. In horror I watched as a routinely patrolling Royal Marine commando stopped in his tracks. From out of the corner of my eye I could see two more heavily armed, green-headed Marines approaching the spot at the double. Zoe did not understand the significance of men wearing green berets and carrying rifles. She did not understand why an open sunroof should cause excitement a few weeks after a Ford Transit with an impromptu sunroof caused a mess in Downing Street. She did not understand why I was leaping up and down and suggesting she should park somewhere else! It was Andy beside her who got the message. A frantic conversation between them and they drove off, just as the imaginary letter I was composing to Zoe's parents had reached the 'I am sorry to tell you . . .' phrase.

We duly met up at the prearranged spot half a mile on from where Zoe had nearly become a guest of the military. The next five miles' walk from Helston was hair-raising. A narrow winding road, thousands of tourist-loaded cars and high hedges preventing both early sight of approaching danger or a quick exit out of the way. From Penhale the road widened out and walking became more tolerable.

A six o'clock that night we reached Lizard Village. Really no more than a collection of souvenir shops. She who does not like walking wanted to do some shopping. He who does not like paying was grateful most of the shops were closed. With an intact bank balance Joan and I carried on to Lizard Point a further mile away.

At half past six we stood at the most southerly point of the British mainland. It was forty-five days since we had left Dunnet Head, 1036 miles of endeavour, an average of twenty-three and a half miles per day despite some of the worst June weather on record. Our emotions were mixed. For Joan, who had wanted desperately to do the 'Furthest North to the Furthest South', it was a moment of supreme achievement. For me, a person to whom logic is sometimes too much of a god, it was satisfying but only a sideshow to the main event. Whatever may be at the furthest north or the furthest south, it is John o'Groats and Land's End that are the definitive, universally recognised points. With one triumph under the belt I was now anxious to return to Helston and rejoin the 'main event'.

That night saw a quiet celebration in Marazion. One objective had been reached, we were only a stones throw from the ulitmate objective, but too much had happened to allow complacency to rear its ugly head.

The next morning, 3 July, we were dropped off at Helston to continue our endeavours to reach Land's End. It all felt a bit of an anti-climax. We had announced to the world at large that we were going to arrive at Land's End on Saturday 6 July and now we did not wish to get there any earlier just in case some well wishers might turn up on that day. This left us three days to walk the remaining thirty-one miles.

Andy and Zoe left us in Helston and returned to Marazion to pack up and move the camp on to St Buryan, six miles from Land's End. Typically it started to rain as we left Helston. It was hot and high humidity made it unpleasantly sticky. We left the main road to walk on quiet side roads through the villages of Sithney and Godolphin Cross. There was a distant rumble of thunder. Joan picked wild flowers from the hedgerows to place later on her father's grave. We reached Marazion and the haze blotted out St Michael's Mount barely half a mile away. Three miles later and it started to rain quite heavily as we reached Penzance. It had been a pleasantly slow amble from Helston; it was only lunch-time but we could see no point in rushing. We rung our back up team, invited them to join us for lunch, and disappeared into a wine bar for the afternoon.

The next day was a relaxed affair, it being almost afternoon before we were dropped off at Penzance. Another slow amble, more rain and we were back in St Buryan. That night we celebrated our forthcoming arrival at Land's End in the St Buryan Inn. It was a nostalgic evening; 440 days earlier we had been celebrating our forthcoming departure from Land's End from the same inn, from the same bar, from the same table. How we missed Iain that night, knowing how he felt just over a year earlier, the trepidation, the excitement. Even our old adversary, the British weather, gave us a fitting finale with a tremendous thunderstorm. The thunder rattled the windows, power was cut off, lightning illuminated the bar, torrents of rain fell outside. I didn't care. Nothing was going to stop us now.

We took the dogs with us that night. Sherry, trembling in mortal fear as the thunder rumbled in from the sea, quivered in a dark corner. Ben, sensing the end was near, quietly sat with his master. Rocky partied to the end. Circulating from table to table he made many friends.

'Nice dog,' said a lady emptying a crisp packet down Rocky's throat.

'Pleasant little fella,' said a nice man, sharing his lunch with our ever appealing mutt.

'Likes his ale,' said the landlord, putting a saucerful of best bitter on the floor for the social climbing canine.

Seeing him cast an appealing eye at another man unwrapping a cigar was too much. 'He doesn't smoke,' I said.

The man looked at his cigar, looked at the handsome harrier and bought him a packet of pork scratchings instead. Rocky wouldn't have looked amiss wearing a bow tie, glass of wine in one paw, cigar in the other. He had made many friends in the last thousand miles and given us all a great deal of pleasure.

The following morning we left our back up team for the last time. With dragging feet we ambled the last six miles, unable to believe that it was all over. Joan gave my last apple to the last horse in Britain and to the melody of the last fart in Britain we carried on. As the portals of the custom house came into view we both started to feel that sadness that comes with the end of a great adventure. At eleven o'clock we arrived at the high cliffs of Land's End. Apart from the local bus company manager there was no welcoming party, friends and family preferring to celebrate with us in the Walnut Tree later that evening. That's how I wanted it. Those moments belonged to Joan an I.

With Zoe and Andy we cracked open the champagne, took the statutory photographs and danced around the signpost. Then Joan and I were alone. No words can describe those moments. If arriving at John o'Groats was only half way, this was the end. I looked at my partner who had been with me for 1067 miles, who had suffered such pain from those horrendous blisters, who had to put up with my moods, my anger, my depression. My partner who does not even like walking but who in two trips walked 2085 miles to help me realise my ambitions. This was our moment of supreme achievement, of supreme togetherness. I did not want those moments to end but they had to sometime. After a few minutes we would go and join our back up team celebrating in the hotel bar. Later that evening we would meet with friends and family in North Petherton and the party would continue well into Sunday.

For now it was moments that no words can describe.